Towards Fairer University Assessment

After all the hours of studying, reading and preparation, the nights spent revising and the writing and re-writing of assignments, 'success' for university students can often be represented with a single grade or digit, summing up a wide range of activities. The authors of this timely book ask how fair that assessment is.

This book is about a long-ignored determinant of student satisfaction, concerning the perception of how fairly students are judged, marked, ranked and rewarded for demonstrating their capabilities at university. In the high-stakes competitive field of higher education, students are increasingly positioned as customers whose views on their university experience are considered vitally important. Yet paradoxically, little research has been undertaken to find out more about how students decide whether they have been treated fairly and what they do about it. This book fills a major gap in our understanding of these issues, responding to four key questions:

- Why is the assessment of students' capabilities the core business of universities?
- What are the main sources of student frustration with assessment arrangements?
- What do students do when they think they have been treated unfairly?
- What can be done to promote fair assessment at university?

In doing so, this book goes beyond the superficial consideration of university assessment as a 'necessary requirement' by unravelling the underlying issues that really count – what is considered fair assessment and what is not.

Towards Fairer University Assessment will be of interest to higher education academics, administrators and managers, researchers in the areas of education policy and politics, as well as advanced undergraduate and postgraduate students.

Nerilee RA Flint is the Education Advisor Student Equity at the Australian National University, Canberra.

Bruce Johnson is Professor of Education at the School of Education, University of South Australia.

Towards Fairer University Assessment

Recognizing the concerns
of students

Nerilee RA Flint and
Bruce Johnson

Routledge
Taylor & Francis Group

LONDON AND NEW YORK

First edition published 2011
by Routledge
2 Park Square, Milton Park, Abingdon, Oxon OX14 4RN

Simultaneously published in the USA and Canada
by Routledge
270 Madison Avenue, New York, NY 10016

Routledge is an imprint of the Taylor & Francis Group, an informa business

© 2011 Nerilee RA Flint and Bruce Johnson

Typeset in Galliard and Gill Sans by
Florence Production Ltd, Stoodleigh, Devon
Printed and bound in Great Britain by
CPI Antony Rowe, Chippenham, Wiltshire

British Library Cataloguing in Publication Data
A catalogue record for this book is available from the British Library

Library of Congress Cataloging-in-Publication Data
Flint, Nerilee, 1961–
    Towards fairer university assessment: recognizing the concerns of
students/Nerilee Flint and Bruce Johnson. – 1st ed.
        p. cm.
    Includes bibliographical references and index.
    1. College students – Rating of – Cross-cultural studies. 2. College
students – Attitudes – Cross-cultural studies. 3. Educational tests
and measurements – Cross-cultural studies. I. Johnson, Bruce,
1951–. II. Title.
    LB2368.F55 2011
    378.1'662 – dc20   2010022491

ISBN13: 978-0-415-57812-7 (hbk)
ISBN13: 978-0-415-57813-4 (pbk)
ISBN13: 978-0-203-83670-5 (ebk)

Contents

Figures

Foreword

... when we went and approached [the lecturer] about [the assignment], she said 'you've got that freedom to do what you want' but she doesn't have a plan of what she wants in the course booklet, so you're not quite sure what she wants. So you do what you think she wants, take into account what she said in class, but then she says 'that's not really what I wanted.' You can't win!

(p. 30)

I do think that anything that is judged ... depending on the mood of the person that is marking it, it can just be not marked in the manner that you would like it marked ... Your destiny is in the hands of someone else depending on how they feel ... that's what I believe sometimes.

(pp. 59–60)

I'm doing this assignment for a reason. I should be getting something out of it; I should be able to take something away from it. I think there should be things that are relevant that you may use later in life.

(p. 75)

Who could criticize the students above for wanting to know what they are expected to present for marking, or for hoping to have it marked professionally and accurately? It also seems reasonable that they would like to engage in meaningful activity and to feel that they are learning something useful. All of these comments raise aspects of fairness. Moreover, the kinds of 'unfairness' that the students allude to are still prevalent in university education, even though we may not speak about them very often. This is an important area of concern, and this book addresses it by demanding that we take the student perspective seriously. Importantly, the authors do not leave the reader in despair but present many useful suggestions for fairer assessment practice. This book is worth reading and the ideas in it are worth applying to our own practice as educators.

I came across the work that forms the basis of this book as a Ph. D. examiner. Nerilee Flint was the Ph. D. candidate and Bruce Johnson was her supervisor. I always enjoy examining Ph. D.s – it is an opportunity to have a dialogue with someone who is as fascinated and passionate as I am about assessment and the student experience. In the UK Ph. D. system there is face-to-face dialogue between candidate and examiners – the viva. Unfortunately this is not the case in the Australian system, where examiners independently make written reports and there is no face-to-face meeting. I say 'unfortunately' not because I think there is any deficiency in the Australian approach, but because at the time I felt disappointed not to be able to meet Nerilee and her supervisor. I knew that we would have had a lot to discuss, agree upon and also challenge each other about. Later on, I did meet Nerilee when she made a trip to Europe, and this was about the time that the book based on her thesis was nearing completion – and I am very pleased that this book has made it to publication. There are few Ph. D. students in my subject area who don't hope to publish a book on the basis of the work that they have been committed to – often for a number of years since they frequently study for a Ph. D. part-time. Few of them do actually publish, for many reasons. 'Life' – many aspects of which have been put on hold during Ph. D. study – takes over; there are pressures from a new academic job; and they face demands to keep up publication counts by producing journal articles. Nerilee and Bruce have obviously formed a great writing team, and this thesis has become an excellent book.

Fairness in educational assessment is a topic of perennial interest. The general public view of assessment in schools and colleges is that it should give everyone a 'fair chance'. For example, it should not be biased or influenced by favouritism. Assessment is, as the authors here point out, seen as a way to promote meritocratic opportunities for all members of society. One view of educational testing, often called the 'scientific measurement' paradigm, has aimed to achieve meritocratic ideals by developing so-called objective tests. Careful question and test construction, and validation through statistical analysis, are deemed to produce testing methods that give 'true' indicators of ability that are unbiased by confounding factors such as social class or ethnicity. This is one view of fairness underpinned by measurement models, and it has been particularly influential in the United States (Wiliam 2006). Meanwhile, more sociologically inclined researchers have been busy demonstrating that tests of this type and many other forms of assessment are *unfair* because of the difficulties that students may face in showing their 'ability' (or potential) due to the poor quality of the education they have experienced, or their lack of social or cultural capital (Filer 2000).

This book acknowledges some of the philosophical and value-based arguments about educational assessment, but it focuses on what happens in the day-to-day context of university study from the student perspective. The authors offer us an insight, in fascinating detail, of students' perceptions of fairness, based on a rigorous and careful research study and a theoretical model derived from the data. The theory of 'demonstrating capability' is an elegant and useful one because it holds together a number of features of assessment – such as task design; information and guidance; marking; procedural matters. These features often appear in bullet point lists in other publications, but without any sense of overall coherence or meaning. If we keep in mind the 'big idea' of the student goal of demonstrating capability, it will help us to make decisions about assessment practice and influence our interactions with students on a day-to-day basis. This book gives us ideas to try out as teachers and assessors. Equally importantly, it paints a vivid picture that brings our own students, so often just faces in a lecture hall, to life. This gives us the inspiration to review what we do and to try to make a positive difference.

Liz McDowell
Professor in Academic Practice, Northumbria University

References

Filer, A (ed.) (2000) *Assessment: social practice and social product*, Routledge, London.
Wiliam, D (2006) 'Assessment for learning: why no profile in US policy?' in *Assessment and learning*, ed. J Gardner, Sage, London, pp. 169–83.

Acknowledgements

We would like to thank the student participants who gave freely of their time, thoughts and experiences of assessment. Without their insights we would not have been able to identify the sources of their frustration, the range of responses they have when they perceive assessment to be unfair, and what influences their responses.

Chapter 1

The importance of fair assessment

Introduction

This book is about a long-ignored determinant of students' satisfaction with their university studies – their perception of how fairly they are judged, marked, ranked and rewarded for demonstrating their capabilities at university. In the high stakes competitive field of higher education, students are increasingly positioned as 'clients' whose views on their university experience are considered vitally important. Yet, paradoxically, little research has been undertaken to find out more about how students decide whether they have been treated fairly, and what they do about it. This book fills a major gap in our understanding of these issues.

The main questions this book addresses are:

- Why is the assessment of students' capabilities the 'core business' of universities?
- What are the main sources of student frustration with assessment arrangements? How do these contribute to global assessments of the 'fairness' of these arrangements? Why does 'fairness' matter so much? What is the link between students' perceptions of the fairness of assessment and their satisfaction with their university studies?
- What do students do when they think they have been treated unfairly? What factors influence how they react? What are the implications of their reactions – for themselves, their teachers and the university?
- What can be done to promote fair assessment at university? Who should be responsible for making university assessment fairer? What changes are possible?

This book goes beyond the superficial consideration of university assessment as a 'toolkit' of tips and tricks by unravelling the underlying issues that really count: what is considered fair assessment and what is not.

This introductory chapter provides the broad policy context in which contemporary universities in Australia, New Zealand, the United Kingdom, the United States and other Western nations operate. Increasingly, universities have become corporations that compete in a global market for research and development funds, high quality staff and, most significantly, for students. In this new era of educational marketization, students are constructed as 'clients' whose 'satisfaction' with what their university offers becomes a major concern. As internal accountability processes seek to ensure high quality teaching and research, students' views on their 'university experience' are now the focus of mandatory end-of-course student evaluations of such things as teaching quality, resources provision and, significantly, assessment arrangements. These student evaluations frequently reveal poor assessment practices that:

- lack authenticity and relevance to real world tasks;
- make unreasonable demands on students;
- are narrow in scope;
- have little long-term benefit;
- fail to reward genuine effort;
- have unclear expectations and assessment criteria;
- fail to provide adequate feedback to students;
- rely heavily on factual recall rather than on higher-order thinking and problem-solving skills.

These inadequacies undermine the credibility of universities and challenge the basic tenets of the liberal meritocratic ideal. As a consequence, there is an urgent need to improve our understanding of students' experiences of assessment, what frustrates and angers them, and what leads them to label some assessment practices as 'unfair'. This chapter provides a strong argument for better assessment practices within universities because *these things matter* in the very competitive, contemporary, higher education marketplace.

In this book we develop the argument that students want the opportunity to demonstrate their capabilities and to have those capabilities recognized. Such opportunity is provided through the process of assessment, and recognition is reflected in the grade or mark they receive for the assessment activities they complete in their courses. Students believe that assessment is unfair if they think that they have not been given the opportunity to demonstrate their capabilities, or if their capabilities have not been recognized. This is the substantive *theory of demonstrating capability*, which explains students' perceptions of the fairness of assessment and their resultant behaviour.

Ultimately, this book's aim is to provide the knowledge base to better understand students' thinking about university assessment and to inform the development of interventions to improve assessment policies and practices in higher education.

Constructions of fairness

From this brief introduction to the book – and its title – it should be obvious that considerations of 'fairness' are inextricably linked to university assessment practices. Yet how communities, and in particular university students, construe such complex notions as 'justice', 'equality' and 'fairness' presents a challenge to non-philosophers (like us) who are trying to understand how 'ordinary' students work through the moral and ethical dimensions of assessment practices in contemporary universities. What follows is a brief foray into the literature on 'fairness' and 'justice'.

Flanagan *et al.* maintain that the stability and viability of social institutions such as universities depend on general 'support in the population for the principles on which the system is based' (2003: 711). In the case of universities, the principles underpinning their essential purposes are based on meritocratic beliefs about distributive justice. These 'popular beliefs' (Marshall *et al.* 1999: 349) are consistent with the widely accepted principle that individuals should be rewarded in the distribution of social status, educational credentials and economic benefits according to their ability and willingness to work hard; they should get what they 'deserve'. While normative philosophers of social justice (e.g. Rawls 1971; Pojman 2001) argue that populist beliefs about 'justice according to deserts' are naïve and simplistic because they ignore the undeserved endowment of 'ability' and 'diligence', many multinational studies of popular beliefs about justice and fairness confirm their widespread appeal (Bjørnskov *et al.* 2009). Marshall *et al.* (1999) discuss the tension between popular or 'consensus' notions of justice and the critiques offered by 'political theorists':

> What they disagree about is what properly counts as the basis of a desert claim. By 'conventional desert claims' we refer to claims, often disputed by philosophers, that people deserve to be rewarded in accordance with things like ability and contribution, irrespective of the extent to which they are responsible for their possession of ability, or for being able to make their contribution.
>
> (1999: 363)

Those same studies confirmed the socially and historically situated nature of popular beliefs about distributive justice by comparing popular beliefs in western-style, capitalist nations (the United States, the UK, Japan and the Netherlands) with those held by populations in post-communist, industrial societies in central and eastern Europe (Millar 1992; Mateju 1997; Flanagan *et al.* 2003). These international comparisons suggest that popular notions of fairness are co-constructed through personal experience and the sharing of social and cultural 'myths' that have their genesis in particular readings of national history.

In Australia, for example, leaders and public commentators regularly invoke the experiences of its soldiers in a flawed military campaign during World War I (at Gallipoli, Southern Turkey, 25 April to 20 December 1915) to explain the origins of key defining features of the Australian psyche: 'standing up for what is right, mateship, courage, teamwork, initiative, belief in a "fair go for all" are traits that stem from Gallipoli. These traits remain as valid today as they did in the last century' (Lieutenant General Ken Gillespie 2010).

Not surprisingly, Australian public opinion polls regularly report strong support (around 90 per cent of respondents) for the view that all Australians deserve a 'fair go' to achieve according to their abilities and the effort they invest, so long as the rewards they get are 'reasonable' (that is, proportional to ability and effort) (Henry 2009). Universities are consistently accorded a pivotal role in this through their assumed application and use of meritocratic processes that reward ability and hard work (Australian National University 2008).

Yet these apparently unproblematic constructions of 'fairness' are confounded by the stark revelation that meritocracies rarely work in the ways described here; there is irrefutable evidence from many studies carried out over the past half century that the simplistic idea that 'ability + effort = success' has little substance in reality (Roper 1970; Pickett and Wilkinson 2010). Too many confounding influences based on social class, race, ethnicity and gender (among other things) expose the meritocratic ideal as a myth or one of Goleman's (1985) bigger 'vital lies' that we share to preserve our faith in the power of individual agency.

But herein lies the 'problem' with studies of the 'fairness' of such things as university assessment; the key considerations are more about perceptions than 'objective' reality. The dilemma we faced in designing and conducting the study that ultimately informed this book was whether to pursue further hard evidence of the existence of inequalities in university assessment or to enter the less well charted realms of student *perceptions* of assessment. We chose the latter because we wanted to *understand* the subjective realities of students as these have been under-researched and underestimated in analyses of the fairness of university assessment. Yet, as we demonstrate throughout the book, students' perceptions are firmly grounded in their assessment experiences so their comments and suggestions to improve university assessment have a practical and immediate relevance for teachers and course leaders. Our aim has always been to challenge some of the tarnished features of academic assessment that have weakened students' belief in the legitimacy of the meritocratic claim in contemporary universities. Like the vast majority of students we work with, we wish to challenge assessment practices that impede the operation of meritocratic processes that are supposed to recognize and reward what we have called 'capability' – that delicate mix of academic ability and personal effort that promotes quality learning. While we know that the meritocratic idea can only be approximated in reality, we have a strong commitment to moving the assessment agenda *towards* a fairer ideal.

While an understanding of 'popular' principles of distributive justice is at the core of our analysis, several other ideas about justice in university settings need to be explored. For example, 'procedural fairness' refers to the perceived fairness of the process used to make assessment decisions. Most definitions refer to the need for clear, well-communicated assessment criteria, the transparent application of those criteria, and the elimination of any bias in the decision-making process. Leventhal (1980), Leventhal *et al.* (1980), and Thibaut and Walker (1975) expand on these 'basic' criteria for 'procedural fairness' to include:

- having the opportunity to voice one's views and arguments during a procedure;
- having the ability to influence the outcome of a procedure;
- being consistent in applying decision-making rules;
- applying procedures based on accurate information;
- having opportunities to appeal the outcome of procedures;
- upholding ethical and moral standards during the process.

These considerations have direct relevance to the fairness judgments of students and will be referred to in Chapter 4 of the book when we analyse how students decide whether they have been treated fairly or unfairly.

A third form of justice relates to the ways students are treated by their teachers. 'Interpersonal justice' relates to the quality of the interactions between students and their teachers. If teachers relate to students in a polite manner, show respect and uphold their dignity, then they are likely to be seen as fairer than teachers who belittle their students, or make negative and damaging remarks about their ability or performance. 'Interpersonal justice' influences students' feelings about their teachers and perhaps means they are more accepting of decisions that otherwise would have been viewed as unfair.

Closely linked to 'interpersonal justice' is a fourth form of justice, 'informational justice', which involves explaining why and how a particular decision is made (Everton *et al.* 2007) and refers to people's perceptions of the fairness of the information used as the basis for making the decision (Greenberg 2005). If students feel that their teachers are open and honest, explain assessment-related details thoroughly and communicate information in a timely manner, then they are likely to be seen as fairer than teachers who do not communicate all of the necessary information, or privilege some students with additional information, or do not explain how an assessment decision is made (for example, lack of feedback related to a grade).

Finally, the notion of 'retributive justice' has some relevance here as it refers to the opportunity to 'put things right' if students can demonstrate, through the application of 'procedural justice' criteria, that they have been unfairly treated. Again, we will refer to this form of justice when we discuss students' options for appealing against grades and applying for their assessment tasks to be re-marked.

In this section, we have briefly ventured into the complex world of moral philosophy to shed light on the meaning and use of key ethical constructs to do with 'fairness'. We have done this to provide some common language and shared understanding about ideas that we will return to in later chapters of the book. We have kept our discussion fairly brief and abstract, knowing that more sophisticated and nuanced understandings will emerge when we use the voices of our participants to identify contradictions and tensions in their thinking that show the complexity and problematic nature of the field.

The policy context: The rise of the neo-liberal university

While thus far we have presented an essentially moral argument for fairer university assessment, we need to acknowledge other powerful forces operating within universities that have their genesis in larger social and economic movements associated with neo-liberalism.

Numerous writers and commentators have contributed to the deconstruction of contemporary higher education policies and practices in 'first world' or advanced economy countries such as the United Kingdom, the United States, Australia and Canada (see, for example, Canaan and Shumar's 2008b edited collection). Most point to the emergence of 'neoliberal practices and structures that are shaping institutions and individuals' (Canaan and Shumar 2008a: 3) in the higher education sector.

It is important to explore these

> neoliberal processes [that] include the infusion of market and competitive logics throughout universities, the rise of audit processes and cultures of accountability, and the replacement of public with private (student and business) funding.
>
> (Dowling 2008: 813)

These processes have infiltrated most aspects of university life and culture to the extent that they are now the 'taken-for-granted', normalized ways of thinking about, doing and evaluating university work. For example, universities readily use the principles of free market competition to justify their implementation of corporatized forms of university management and governance to promote institutional efficiency and accountability. They involve the use of sophisticated and widespread audit processes to promote the 'quality' of universities to make them competitive in the marketplace for the 'best' students, most productive staff and largest research grants. This inevitably involves the use of 'performance management' processes with staff in which quite narrow 'outcomes' measures are applied to gauge the extent to which staff contribute to the achievement of corporate goals. Along with a set of metrics that show the performance of staff in research (total amount of research money won, rating of the quality of the funding source, total number of peer-reviewed publications, and the rating of the status of the journals in which the papers were published), new measures of teaching effectiveness are being applied that draw on student evaluations of courses (using the Australian Course Evaluation Instrument, for example; Scott 2006) and teaching (using local Student Evaluation of Teaching instruments). These implicate assessment practices in what Lyotard (1984) and Ball (2003) would call unquestioned and imposed regimes of narrow performativity. They strongly influence appointment processes in universities and are used to reward 'successful' staff (and penalize 'non-performing' staff) through formal promotion processes and, increasingly, access to study leave, conference attendance and internal research grants.

While these overt processes are the most obvious manifestations of neo-liberalism in our universities, more pervasive, internalized self-disciplining mechanisms work towards 'creating for ourselves a neoliberal academic subjectivity' in which the logic and discourses of competition, individualism and self-promotion become 'internalised and normalised' (Dowling 2008: 813). Citing other writers on academic identity formation, Dowling constructs a convincing explanation of this process:

> Lawrence Berg (in Castree *et al.*, 2006) provides a specific example of how this neoliberal academic subjectivity may be created, suggesting that the CV is more than the 'objective' record of achievements. For Berg, the CV is a technique for disciplining the self, to align the body with the objectives of the institution, a means by which we insert 'our bodies within a disciplinary grid of rewards and punishment constituted in liberal academia' (p. 765). Auditing and accountability, key processes in the production of a neoliberal self, are manifest in the academy in research and teaching audit processes. According to Loftus (2006), these processes produce a domination of things (publications, stars) over people and 'a system of self discipline that pits academic against academic' (p. 111).
>
> (2008: 813)

If these external and internal mechanisms of governance work in the ways proposed, the implications for university teachers are quite profound. Clearly, questions about the quality of university assessment cannot be ignored by universities themselves (to do so would jeopardize their market-driven project to be 'competitive') or by university teachers (to do so would make them vulnerable in performance audits). These very pragmatic, policy-driven considerations explain why *assessment matters* in neo-liberal universities.

The student perspective

With students positioned as clients of universities and consumers of their goods and services by the rhetoric of the marketplace, what *they* think about assessment also matters. Considerable research has established that assessment is important to students in universities (Brown and Knight 1994; Brown 1997; Brown and Glasner 1999; Rust 2002; Ramsden 2003; Bryan and Clegg 2006; Biggs and Tang 2007; Boud and Falchikov 2007). For example, Scott (2006) found that assessment was identified as a key area for improvement within 14 Australian universities when the qualitative comments of nearly 95,000 graduates were examined using the data analysis tool CEQuery.

Assessment is also the most powerful lever teachers have to influence both the way students behave as learners and their response to courses. Qualitative studies 'of the way students respond to assessment, or at least to their perceptions of assessment provide a vivid insight into its central importance in their lives' (Gibbs 1999: 42). What students learn is closely connected to what is assessed. The assessment methods employed by teachers encourage students to learn in certain ways, as students mostly study what they think will be assessed.

Many studies have shown that students are very strategic in how they approach their courses, and the way that assessment is set up influences what they learn, including whether they take a surface or deep approach to learning. Brown and Knight suggest that assessment 'defines what students regard as important, how they spend their time, and how they come to see themselves as students' (1994: 12). Thus the assessment system is the dominant influence on the way students learn; assessment drives learning (McCoubrie 2004), and it defines the curriculum for students (Ballantyne *et al.* 1997). Assessment is also intricately connected to student motivation, and a high level of motivation is necessary for learning (Crooks 1988).

Because assessment is so central to students' experience of university life, we have consciously 'privileged' students' perspectives over those of university teachers and administrators. This has involved widespread and prolonged engagement with students to provide them with opportunities to share their experiences, perceptions, attributions, feelings and ideas for change. We have accepted students' contributions largely at face value without too quickly moving to pass our own judgments on the veracity of their perspectives. We think that it is timely to pause and let students' 'voices' be heard in an environment in which the power dynamics between teachers and students have changed significantly since students asserted their 'rights' during the late 1960s and early 1970s. The competitive, individualized culture of contemporary universities undermines 'student voice', so we believe an initiative like ours that enables students to articulate their views adds a level of understanding about assessment issues that is currently missing or undervalued.

Structure of the book

This book draws on research conducted at the University of South Australia. Chapter 2 provides a description and justification of that work – an in-depth qualitative study of students' views of assessment arrangements at our university. Selected students were interviewed over a three-year period using a variety of techniques to elicit their complex views on the fairness of assessment. An iterative approach to study design was employed involving cycles of simultaneous data collection and analysis that informed the next round of data collection. Details are provided of the ways data were managed and analysed using an applied grounded theory approach.

The subsequent chapters in the book draw extensively on the data from this study to identify the sources of student frustration with assessment, what criteria they use to establish the fairness and unfairness of assessment, and how they respond when they feel unfairly treated.

Chapter 3 deals with the sources of students' frustration with assessment. For students to have a chance to be successful at university, they need to know and understand what is required by assessment tasks and what their teachers expect of them; not knowing or not understanding either of these contributes to feelings of frustration. Despite the widespread use of course booklets to inform students of assessment requirements, many students still feel confused about assessment tasks and the expectations of teaching staff.

In this chapter we identify and discuss the most significant sources of frustration including:

- unclear assessment criteria;
- unclear expectations;
- uncertainty about how and why a grade is assigned to an assessment piece;
- ambiguity over 'word counts';
- inconsistently applied deadlines;
- lack of opportunities to demonstrate *capability*.

By detailing these sources of frustration, we are able to identify those aspects of assessment that can be readily changed to improve students' levels of satisfaction with their university experience.

In Chapter 4, we analyse the complex processes students use to decide whether assessment practices are fair. We describe the individual and shared thinking processes students use to make sense of their assessment experiences. In deciding the fairness of assessment, students draw on their own and others' past experiences of assessment to define a set of 'fairness' criteria. Students deem assessment to be fair if it satisfies the following criteria:

- It is conducted on a 'level playing field' where none of the competing students has an advantage at the outset of the assessment activity.

In practice, this means that work is marked on its merits, there is consistency in marking, and there is consistency of information about assessment arrangements.

- Students receive feedback that justifies or explains a grade, including suggestions about how to improve the grade.
- Students are given a variety of relevant assessment tasks to demonstrate their capability. Perceptions of relevance are strongly tied to what students think is valued in the workplace.
- Students are taught by competent, skilled and caring staff who are approachable, display empathy, engage with students and assist them with their work.

Throughout the chapter, we discuss how these fairness criteria link to broader notions of distributive, procedural, interpersonal, informational and retributive justice.

In Chapter 5, we explore what students do after they have made a judgment about the fairness of assessment. How do they feel when they believe they have been treated unfairly? How do they respond? What actions do they take?

The emotional responses of students can be quite profound and long lasting. Students reported feeling 'useless', 'annoyed', 'sad', 'totally pissed off', 'resentful', 'cheated', 'cross' and 'demoralized'. Yet the decision to take action to address perceived unfairness is influenced by a number of personal and contextual factors including:

- the students' levels of desperation;
- concerns about the ramifications of taking action;
- students' levels of self-confidence, and sense of self-efficacy;
- their knowledge of grievance processes;
- their past experiences.

Students' responses cluster around three groups of actions: 'opting out', 'surviving' and 'taking action'. These groups of actions are unpacked in detail in Chapter 5 and depict the full range of coping strategies used by students to deal with their perceptions of unfair assessment.

The first group of responses represents the most serious and damaging consequences of poor assessment practices: students' partial or complete withdrawal from university life. This revelation helps to explain why student attrition rates are around 30 per cent per year in most OECD (Organisation for Economic Co-operation and Development) universities.

The second group of responses involves learning to 'live with' the reality of unfair assessment. Students who adopt these responses avoid interacting with teaching staff, skip classes and, in some cases, accept a failing grade and repeat a course just to 'get through' their degree. They seek solace from other aggrieved students, engage in blame shifting away from their own performance to that of their teachers and invoke coping mantras such as 'just going with the flow' and 'just wearing it'.

The final group of responses involves more assertive and 'rational' actions, ranging from seeking more feedback from staff or seeking a re-mark to lodging a formal appeal against an assessment decision.

In the final chapter of the book, we summarize the key findings presented in earlier chapters and explore their implications for teaching staff, course coordinators, programme teams and university policy developers. We present numerous practical recommendations to increase students' and teachers' understanding of assessment issues, and to promote the adoption of assessment policies and practices that are fair and equitable.

Who this book is for

When we initially thought of writing and publishing a book on university assessment, we were aware of the need for a text that was directed at university teachers who were *not* experts in educational assessment but who wanted to expand their understanding of some fundamental issues about assessment. We chose to privilege the voices of students to access a previously silenced and hidden perspective on university assessment. We think that this emphasis on students' views about the fairness of assessment offers university teachers *and students* new insights into what frustrates students and, as a consequence, what can be done to prevent or alleviate these alienating and destructive feelings. Consequently, we wrote the book with two 'typical' audiences in mind: university teachers and students.

University teachers who read this book are likely to:

- be employed as university teachers with responsibilities to assess and grade their students in accordance with university policies;
- embrace 'popular' conceptions of meritocratic justice in which academic ability and effort are recognized and rewarded through assessment schemes at university;
- be aware of some of the criticisms of university assessment processes raised by students and employers and be motivated to investigate their veracity more closely;
- have some interest in the moral justifications for making university assessment fairer but will not have an abiding interest in deep philosophical issues;
- be experiencing some of the accountability pressures that arise in neo-liberal universities because of rising expectations for 'quality' outcomes;
- feel some professional responsibility for the learning and well-being of their students;
- have some commitment to improving their assessment practices in the light of what is presented here.

Students who read this book are likely to:

- embrace 'popular' conceptions of meritocratic justice in which academic ability and effort are recognized and rewarded through assessment schemes at university;
- have had negative personal experiences of university assessment;
- have an interest in being better informed about university assessment;
- support initiatives to change assessment practices;
- accept some personal responsibility for taking action to respond to perceived unfair assessment.

At this point it is probably timely to point out who this book is not written for – researchers and academics who specialize in complex philosophical and sociological analysis and debate about social justice, equity and fairness in contemporary societies. We readily acknowledge the existence of longstanding, persistent and unfair inequalities in educational outcomes that result in particular groups in society having greater access to university study than other groups. Like many of our colleagues, we have spent most of our academic careers trying to understand how the schooling system is implicated, in both overt and subtle ways, in the perpetuation of social inequalities. We have read and valued the seminal work of social and cultural reproduction researchers and theorists like Bernstein (1971) in the UK, Bowles and Gintis (1976) in the United States and Fitzgerald (1976) in Australia. We have also accessed recent research into the possibilities of early interventions in low socioeconomic status schools that focus on the four 'conditions of entry' to university: availability, accessibility, achievement and aspiration (see Gale *et al.* 2010).

However, we believe that a detailed re-examination of these fundamental issues is beyond the scope of a book that seeks to look *within* universities to identify how students' constructions of fairness in assessment influence how they feel and behave. This is not to diminish the importance of these issues but simply to acknowledge that they are better addressed by other authors in other places.

Conclusion

Assessment is the 'core business' of universities. Despite this, many assessment practices are ineffectual, limiting, irrelevant and blatantly unfair. In this introductory chapter we have laid the foundation for an in-depth examination of the sources of student frustration with their university assessment, how they apply complex and sometimes contradictory ideas about what is 'fair' and 'just' within meritocratic institutional settings, and what they do – and do not do – as relatively powerless actors in the assessment process. In doing so, we have revealed our commitment to exposing assessment practices that compromise the achievement of a more meritocratic ideal in universities, and to providing the rationale and starting point for significant reforms to assessment in universities.

Chapter 2

Researching students' perceptions of fair assessment

A qualitative approach

Students respond to the situation they perceive, and it is not necessarily the same situation that we have defined. It is imperative to be aware of this routine divergence between intention and actuality in higher education teaching . . . becoming aware of it is part of what it means to teach well.

(Ramsden 2003: 63)

The criteria I had identified and applied to other work seemed not to apply in this case, and I couldn't understand why. I guess I had developed a strong capacity for self-assessment and felt resentment at the injustice I perceived to be taking place, I remember discussing the matter with peers, raising the issue and getting nowhere.

(Falchikov in Boud and Falchikov 2007: 7)

Assessment is important, fairness is important and perceptions are important. There is an urgent need to understand students' experiences of assessment better, what frustrates and angers them, and what leads them to label some assessment practices as 'unfair'. In this book we present a comprehensive understanding of what undergraduate university students perceive to be fair and unfair assessment.

To understand students' perceptions of assessment we draw on research conducted at the University of South Australia. The objective of the study was to elicit and make sense of students' perceptions of the fairness of assessment. This required hearing students' stories regarding their assessment experiences. An iterative approach to study design was employed involving cycles of simultaneous data collection and analysis that informed the next round of data collection.

Using an applied grounded theory approach, we developed a *substantive theory of demonstrating capability*, which explains undergraduate university students' perceptions of the fairness of assessment. The subsequent chapters in the book draw extensively on this study to identify the sources of student frustration with assessment, what criteria they use to establish the fairness and unfairness of assessment and how they respond when they feel unfairly treated.

In this chapter, we outline the processes of collecting and managing the data from numerous interviews with students. We describe recruitment and sampling methods, along with the profile of students interviewed. We explain the interview process as it evolved, and the management of the resulting data. We then turn to an explanation of the data analysis and how that contributed to the development of the grounded theory. Finally, we establish the quality and integrity of the theory using Glaser and Strauss (1967) and Glaser's (1978, 1992) criteria of work, fit, relevance and modifiability.

Ethics and consent

Ethical considerations were an important aspect of this study because Nerilee, who conducted the interviews, was a teacher in the school in which the study was conducted. To avoid setting up a power differential, we chose to recruit and interview students who were not in Nerilee's classes.

The study was explained to all teachers in the school and, without exception, all were supportive. The identities of students, teachers, courses, programmes and schools were not revealed in the interview transcripts. Students were given pseudonyms, while teachers were assigned a random letter of the alphabet, preceded by 'lecturer' or 'tutor' – for example, 'lecturer X'.

Recruitment of participants

Selected students were interviewed over a three-year period using a variety of techniques to elicit their complex views on the fairness of assessment. Four rounds of interviews were conducted, each with a different method of recruitment due to the sampling technique being employed and the success rate of earlier methods. As grounded theorists seek power and relevance in concepts rather than a statistically valid representative sample, we did not have a particular number of students in mind before beginning the interviews.

In recruiting for the *first round* of interviews, we described the nature and purposes of the study to second- and third-year students at the beginning of lectures in core courses of one programme. An information sheet and consent form were placed in the pigeonholes of a random selection of students, asking them to consider being interviewed. As a result, three students were interviewed and initial themes were developed from the transcript data. These will be discussed later in the chapter.

Recruitment for the *second round* of students was similar to the first round. We introduced the study to other classes of students and began to use the technique of purposeful sampling; we made a calculated decision to sample according to a preconceived set of dimensions (Glaser 1992). We sought a variety of students in terms of age, gender and year level – and therefore variation in life experiences at school and university.

This resulted in another nine interviews with students from one pro-gramme. Having reached a point where interviews with additional students were not yielding new insights, we began theoretical sampling (Glaser 1978; Glaser and Strauss 1967). This involved us checking the emergent conceptual framework and consciously seeking data from new students. This process is not a form of verification but rather a way of utilizing the emergent theory to develop it further. At this point we broadened the selection pool to include students from another programme taught within the same school. We also included honours students from both programmes in the hope that they could offer a different perspective, and at one point we sought students who were less successful at university. These processes were used to recruit eight more students, making a total of twenty.

A *third round* of interviews was undertaken after this data was analyzed. Four more students were interviewed. Here, we again used theoretical sampling, approaching three students: two self-declared 'low achievers' and a third student who was referred to us by a colleague. This last student had spoken to a colleague about a range of serious issues related to assessment and a particular teacher with whom he was having difficulty. The two 'low-achieving' students had spoken very highly of this teacher; we were thus intrigued with how one teacher could bring out such opposing viewpoints. The fourth student in this third round of interviews was recruited via an email request that we had circulated, appealing to students to contact us to participate in an interview if they had issues with assessment, particularly with receiving final course grades that were a bare pass, a fail, or if they had received a mark for an assessment item that was very different from what they had expected.

A final, *fourth round* of interviews was conducted during the writing stage of the research. This is often the case in grounded theory research, as much of the development of the theory occurs during the writing stage. To recruit students we employed a different strategy again. We described aspects of the developing theory to a class of students who had not had anything to do with the study to date, omitting all details related to the part of the theory we wanted to speak with students about. Following this we circulated an email to the internal and external students studying the course. This resulted in eight interviews: two by telephone, and six by a series of emails.

Another two students from different courses, who had heard of the study from peers and had issues with assessment, approached us to be interviewed around the same time we were conducting this fourth round of interviews. A total of 34 students were interviewed for the study.

Profile of students

To maintain the anonymity of the programmes and courses involved, the following description of the profile of students is intentionally general.

Utilizing the broad fields of education prescribed by the Australian Government Department of Education, Science and Training (DEST), the students came from a total of nine different programmes within the categories of 'Management and Commerce', 'Society and Culture' and 'Agriculture, Environmental and Related Studies'.

The students interviewed ranged in age from 19 to 42 years, with nearly half under 22 years of age. There were 21 females and 13 males interviewed. Most students were in second or third year, although four students were completing a fourth year, with three studying honours and one in the fourth year of a double degree.

The weighted average mark (WAM) for the first 20 students ranged from 53 to 90 (100 being the highest possible WAM). We asked the final 14 students to describe themselves as low, mid or high achievers. While it was not important to know the exact WAM at this stage of the development of the theory, it was useful to know how they viewed themselves.

Interviews

Each interview lasted between 50 and 70 minutes, apart from the initial three, which took 40–45 minutes. Grounded theory interviewing differs from much in-depth interviewing (Chenitz 1986; Charmaz 2006), and this was evident in our interviews, where a narrower range of topics were used in subsequent interviews as we looked to gather specific data informed by the analysis of earlier interviews.

In *round one*, the interviews were semi-structured, incorporating some free-flowing questions aimed at gaining a general understanding of students' different perspectives on the topic (Bogdan and Biklen 1992; Minichiello *et al.* 1995). Students were invited to discuss a range of matters related to assessment. Typical questions included:

- In what (if any) situations had students felt they had experienced unfairness in assessment?
- What would be necessary for assessment to be fair?
- Did the students talk with each other about assessment issues?
- What action had students taken when they felt something was unfair?
- What is the connection between learning and assessment?
- What role did assessment play in their lives?

The *round two* interviews were semi-structured, but included a series of vignettes that encouraged students to reveal more about their assessment experiences. As this was a crucial stage in the data collection, we digress here to explain in more detail the use of vignettes: what they are, when they are used, and how they were used in this research. Following this, we will return to the description of the final two rounds of interviews.

The use of vignettes

Vignettes are usually brief descriptions of hypothetical people or situations. They have been used in many forms of research, particularly social science research, in qualitative and quantitative studies. Vignette materials are particularly useful for obtaining data on people's beliefs (Farwell and Weiner 1996) and have traditionally been used to study issues related to ethics and justice. They have often been used when dealing with topics that are sensitive, diverse examples being: evaluating children's personal safety knowledge (Johnson 2000); students' perceptions of cheating (Ashworth et al. 1997); children's perceptions of appropriate work strategies in classroom settings (Nelson-Le Gall and Scott-Jones 1985); whether white people in the United States are averse to living in integrated neighbourhoods (John and Bates 1990); perceptions of appropriate punishments for convicted offenders (Miller et al. 1986); public attitudes and values related to whether people would recommend the continuation or termination of expensive care with limited medical value (Denk et al. 1997); risk behaviours of individuals who inject drugs (McKeganey et al. 1996); and conflict in the caring relationship of elderly people with their female caregivers (Rahman 1996).

In much research using vignettes, the respondents receive the same vignettes, to which they are then asked to respond. Responses may be gathered in a variety of ways: obtaining answers to a standard question after exposure to a vignette, where respondents have to rate their answer; conducting in-depth interviews; seeking fixed-choice responses and using an open-ended question; or from completing a questionnaire. In our study students were asked to comment on the vignettes, and sometimes they were specifically asked to discuss any issues of fairness.

It was very appropriate to use vignettes in this study because, as with previous studies using the technique, we were tackling a sensitive issue, dealing with beliefs, and attempting to understand what individuals do in response to what they perceive to be unfair treatment – that is, unfair assessment.

To develop the vignettes, we sought ideas from the initial three interviews. We reflected on issues related to fairness from our own teaching and learning experiences, and spoke with teachers to elicit their thoughts about what they felt students' fairness issues were. As more interviews were conducted, we had a growing body of students' comments to reflect upon to develop authentic vignettes, and students were also asked, within the interview, to design a vignette. Approximately 12 vignettes were developed, some of which are included in the box on p. 18.

Vignette 1

Mary, Jane, Rob and Sam are put in a group by the lecturer to do an assignment.

Mary does not contribute much at all. She misses some meetings and doesn't do what she is meant to do. In an attempt at fairness the lecturer gets the students to sit down at the end and divide 20 marks up between the group according to their participation in the group effort. They have to support their division with comments and examples. This is done anonymously and handed up to the lecturer who takes it into account for the final mark.

As a result of this Mary gets a lower grade than everyone else.

VIGNETTE 1A

Mary claims the group arranged meetings at times she couldn't make and when she wasn't there she was given tasks that no one else wanted to do – she didn't want to do those tasks either, so she didn't.

Vignette 2

In the first lecture of a course all students are told that they cannot consult with the lecturer on an individual basis. Everyone is being treated equally.

To help with questions related to assessment items some time is devoted to student questions in tutorial sessions. The people taking the tutorials are not necessarily the lecturer. The lecturer designs the assessment tasks.

Vignette 3

A tutorial group meets once a week for discussion. Students are meant to read set articles before tutorials so they can contribute to the discussion. This all leads to a paper that gets written and assessed.

Some students never contribute. Laura is doing the readings but is too nervous to speak; John is doing the readings but doesn't think his ideas are very good so won't speak. Jill/Jack is not doing the readings but is taking notes during the discussion and getting ideas for the upcoming paper.

Vignette 4

Jane/John works extremely hard on an assignment. She/he gets it back with a grade and two words written on it.

VIGNETTE 4A

What if the grade was HD [high distinction] and the two words were 'Outstanding work'?

VIGNETTE 4B

Jane/John rushes an assignment, hardly putting in any effort at all. She/he gets it back with a grade and two words written on it.

Holstein and Gubrium (1995) present the view that researchers need to consider interviews as part of the thought-making and construction processes of the interviewees: part of the meaning-making process. Compared with conventional semi-structured interviews, vignettes helped to enliven, stimulate and cultivate the interpretive capabilities of the students.

Holstein and Gubrium (1995) also claim that asking a person to address a topic from one point of view, then another, is a way of activating a respondent's stock of knowledge, of exploring the various ways in which the respondent attaches meaning to the phenomena under investigation. This technique was used with vignettes. After eliciting a student's response to a particular vignette (for example, Vignette 1), Nerilee would continue the story with a bit more information, presenting a different point of view (Vignette 1A). This prompted students to look at the situation from a different perspective.

Final rounds of interviews

Having discussed the use of vignettes in the second round of interviews, we now return to a brief description of the final two rounds of interviews.

By the *third round* of interviews, we had well-developed categories from the data analysis and a partially developed theory. We asked more specific questions and there was a focus on some critical aspects of the topic. As Glaser (2001) states, grounded theory researchers are able to vary questions as they develop the theory.

In the *fourth round* of interviews, students were recruited to speak about one aspect of the theory: their responses to unfair assessment – that is, what they actually did about it. By the end of this fourth round of interviews we felt we had enough data to finalize our theory.

Transcription

Glaser (1998) offers sound advice to grounded theory researchers not to tape interviews, on the premise that grounded theory is not about description; it is about producing a theory that exists on a conceptual level and is composed of integrated hypotheses (Glaser 2001). Glaser advocates taking copious field notes after interviews or observation sessions, and states that taping undermines the power of grounded theory methodology to delimit the research quickly. From our experience, taping definitely results in the collection of more data than is necessary, but it is a brave qualitative researcher who would choose not to record interviews.

We taped and transcribed the first 20 interviews from *round one* and *round two*. *Round three* interviews were audiotaped and selectively transcribed because we were looking for specific data by this stage and did not need to transcribe the complete interview. *Round four* interviews varied. It was not necessary to have detailed records of all that was said in terms of developing the theory at this point. The face-to-face interviews were again audiotaped and selectively transcribed. During telephone interviews Nerilee took copious notes, which is one advantage of using a non-visual medium. Email interviews were printed and effectively became transcripts.

The decision to vary the interview style and recording techniques is consistent with a grounded theory approach in which the research agenda evolves as the theory emerges (Glaser and Strauss 1967; Glaser 1978; Charmaz 2006).

Reflective journal

As with many qualitative studies, we used reflective journals for many purposes. These ranged from clarifying thoughts about the interviews to commenting on anything that seemed relevant at the time, including points to think about or investigate further. We also used journals to record relevant conversations with students outside the interview situation and general or specific observations that we thought could inform the study. We also recorded sampling decisions and day-to-day logistics connected to the research.

The use of literature in this research

We began this study by searching for literature on research that addressed the focus of the study: students' perceptions of the fairness of assessment. We found it had not been dealt with in depth. This influenced the decision to use grounded theory as the methodology to investigate the topic. As Stern suggests, 'the strongest case for the use of grounded theory is in investigations of relatively unchartered [sic] waters, or to gain a fresh perspective in a familiar situation' (1980: 20). As the study progressed and we continued searching the literature, we found that the topic had been part of other research (for example: Sambell et al. 1997; Houston and Bettencourt 1999), but nowhere had it been the main focus.

Finding a scarceness of information on the topic, we turned to literature on assessment, fairness and perceptions of fairness. Once the analysis was in progress, and we realized what other literature to seek, we read literature relevant to the developing theory. For example, it was necessary in the early stages of analysis to gain a greater understanding of students' reasons for not objecting or protesting in situations that to us seemed quite unfair. To develop our understanding we read about power relations, focusing on the work of Michel Foucault (1977, 1980) and various commentators on his work (Rabinow 1984; Walkerdine 1990; McHoul and Grace 1993; Gore 1995; Marshall 1996; Canaan 1997; Steinberg 1997; Barker 1998; Southgate 2000).

We also accessed the literature on organizational justice, which raised a number of questions that helped us develop our theory further. These questions included: What do students take into account when deciding whether a grade they are awarded is fair or unfair? What procedures or processes are important to them? Is it possible that students at university are making decisions to continue with courses, programmes or even university based on perceptions of fairness? What do students do if they perceive unfairness? If workplace colleagues often co-construct different perceptions of fairness through discussion, could the same be said for students in a university?

During the final stages of analysis and once the theory was well developed, we sought literature related to the various aspects of the theory. We drew relevant extant knowledge from a variety of disciplines, including education, organizational behaviour, organizational psychology and management studies. Its inclusion helps to embed the substantive theory in wider bodies of knowledge.

Category development

Initial themes

To get a feel for the data, we studied transcripts from the first three interviews and the journal entries. From these, we established seven general themes:

- There is a level of acceptance, or tolerance, by students that certain aspects of assessment are unfair. This was highlighted by, but not limited to, discussion on group assessment and lack of detail in some course outlines.
- Students perceive the purpose of assessment to be very narrow – as a test of their learning, a way of ranking them.
- Students believe assessment items control their learning. If a task or learning activity is not part of an assessment item, students will not view it as an essential part of their learning.
- Teachers are considered to be powerful. Generally the decisions they make about grades are discussed by students but not challenged.
- It appears that students have little awareness or knowledge of university assessment policies and procedures.
- Discussion, particularly with other students, influences perceptions of fairness. Students often talk with each other about grades to make comparisons and confirm or decide whether they think they have received an unfair grade. Some students will follow this up with the teacher afterwards but not necessarily divulge that they think they have been unfairly marked.
- When course outlines do not provide detailed assessment criteria, students think that it is unfair when teachers provide supplementary information about assessment to only a few students.

Within these themes there was much complexity and variation. Reflecting on the themes, we knew a lot was not being said. Listening to students speaking in the corridors, at bus stops and on field trips had revealed much more than these first three interviews. We were concerned that perhaps students were worried about speaking about their issues, concerns and opinions, or perhaps they were nervous in the interviews. A journal entry at the time outlines this concern:

> Get the students to broaden what they talk about – beyond marking – or is marking all they consider when thinking of fair assessment? Haven't had any talking about extensions and variations among teachers in an interview, have outside of interview situation – e.g. paddling around West Lakes one of my students brought the topic up – he knew I had interviewed Duncan (as Duncan had told him) and he said Duncan had told him he had 'some things to say', as if Duncan had made some really important points about things that were unfair. I hadn't thought Duncan was too phased about anything – either Duncan didn't say what he had planned to – or perhaps he speaks in a really casual way about things that are important to him.

To encourage students to reveal more, it was at this point that vignettes were used in interviews.

Determining the core category

Detailed coding and analysis of data began after completing nearly 20 interviews. The transcribed files were imported into QSR International N6 (2002) software, which was used for coding most of the interviews. Each line, sentence or paragraph was examined depending on the complexity of the data. Hundreds of initial codes were identified in this open coding stage. Open coding refers to the initial fracturing of data, and selective coding is the coding that is undertaken once a core variable is found.

After much analysis we were able to decide on the core variable, or core category. This is the category that relates to as many other categories as possible and reoccurs frequently in the data. We decided the core category was 'demonstrating capability'.

Development of a basic social process

Having decided on the core category we recognized that it was not static; it was a process. 'Demonstrating capability' was a basic social process (BSP), a particular type of core category with two or more clear, emergent stages. We returned to the data to re-check and refine all of the categories until the stages of the BSP were clear. We drew up many versions of the basic social process until the categories were condensed into the fewest number that could explain the greatest amount of variation in the behaviour of the students. This is referred to in grounded theory as 'category reduction' (Glaser 1978: 125). We refined the categories further as we wrote about the theory.

The merging of data collection, writing and final analysis is quite typical in grounded theory methodology, and interviews continued until we felt our theory was 'complete'.

Measures to ensure the integrity of the theory

In this section we describe the measures we took to ensure the fit, work, relevance and modifiability of the theory – that is, the criteria Glaser and Strauss (1967) and Glaser (1978, 1992) recommend when evaluating a grounded theory and assessing its integrity. When these criteria are met, a theory provides a conceptual approach to action and change.

Does the theory fit?

When the theory reflects the data rather than any preconceived hypotheses or concepts it is deemed to 'fit'. Fit 'is another word for validity' (Glaser 1978: 18).

In this study, fit was established by initially coding incidents identified in each interview, and comparing newly emerging codes until bigger categories were developed. These categories were built up and rearranged as each subsequent interview was examined. This was continued until no new concepts or categories were found, and at the end of the third round of interviews, we felt we had delimited the theory; we had condensed the categories into the minimum number that could explain the greatest amount of variation in behaviour of the university students. Once we had identified the basic social process, we re-examined a number of the transcripts taken from various stages of the study to ascertain whether anything had been missed.

To satisfy the criteria of fit, Glaser states that the theory will 'fit the realities under study in the eyes of the subjects, practitioners and researchers in the area' (1992: 15). Bearing this in mind, we presented the findings to a small number of people we felt had varied but strong connections to the topic: a student counsellor, three teachers from completely different sections of the university than that in which the study was conducted, and a student advisory officer employed by the university's student association. Without exception, the feedback from all these individuals was that it made absolute sense – that it resonated with them, and that they had never considered it in such a comprehensive way before.

Despite this endorsement, a fourth round of interviews was conducted to explore further the students' responses to unfair assessment in greater detail.

Within the same week we presented the theory to teachers in a School of Education seminar series, and to the chair of a divisional teaching and learning committee. Again, the feedback was that the theory made complete sense.

We had not initially planned to present the theory to groups of students; however, we found the responses late in the process of writing the theory illuminating. As a result, we presented the theory to two focus groups of students whose brief was to interject, comment, question, criticize and seek clarification. The first group was made up of four students: two in the final weeks of a three-year degree, and two in the final weeks of their second year. The second group comprised two students who were in first year but who had partially completed studies in another tertiary institution before attending university. In each of these 90-minute focus group sessions, students made many comments and suggestions. Every point they made had been covered in the theory.

It is important to note that the students in the focus groups had not been interviewed in the study. We were not attempting to check or test the validity of the theory in the eyes of the interviewees. As Glaser warns, participants 'may or may not understand, or even like the theory' you develop (2001: 11). Moreover, the theory itself 'is not their voice, it is a generated abstraction from their doings and its meaning which are taken as data for the generation' of the theory. However, seeking the feedback of these other students was a worthwhile process as it confirmed that it made sense to them.

Does the theory work?

If a theory works, it will explain the major variations in behaviour of the people as they attempt to resolve their main concern or problem, in this case the sources of frustration with assessment. If the theory 'works' it can also be used to predict and interpret what may happen in the field of study. According to Glaser and Strauss the substantive theory 'must enable the person who uses it to have enough control in everyday situations to make its application worth trying' (1967: 245).

The feedback from a wide range of individuals confirmed that the theory does explain the variations in the assessment-related behaviour of students: in Glaser's terms, the theory 'works'. A typical comment from a student was: 'I hadn't thought of it in that way but it makes complete sense,' and from a teacher: 'It is far more complex than I had ever thought but I can now see where students are coming from.'

A theory has power when it explains, predicts and interprets the processes operating in the field of study. The theory we have developed has considerable explanatory power because it was constructed from the constant comparative process and the merging of categories until all variables found in the data were included. This power was also partly achieved by using descriptive labels that are simple, meaningful and make sense to others; labels that we carefully constructed, reworked and modified by analysing the data until they were indicative of the information contained within them.

Is the theory relevant?

Relevance is achieved if a grounded theory fits and works, and if it offers explanations of the problems in the field of study. If a theory is forced or preconceived and not grounded in the data, it will not achieve relevance because it fails to explain the problems or basic processes in the field of study. To that end, the theory we have developed has achieved relevance.

Is the theory modifiable?

Glaser's final criteria for judging the integrity of a grounded theory addresses whether the theory is modifiable: will the theory continue to fit, work and be relevant as time passes and conditions change, and will it be applicable to other similar fields of study? A grounded theory needs to account for variation. It must be written at such a level of conceptualization that it is flexible enough to accommodate additional properties and categories if new data present variations to what has already been constructed. If the theory remains at a descriptive level of the substantive area, it will not have the requisite flexibility. A change in dimensions of time or space should not invalidate a grounded theory; it is simply altered. Its longevity is thus ensured.

It was never the intention of this study to represent all student groups; however, we note that the most obvious absences from the subject sample are students from natural and physical sciences, engineering and related technologies, and creative arts. We believe that the theory we present here is flexible enough to take into account perceptions of students from the groups that have not been represented. Although inclusion of new data in the process of ongoing comparison might result in slight alterations to a component of the theory, the theory we have generated will not be invalidated because it does not just draw on the insights of the 32 students studied here; it takes our understanding from a descriptive level to a conceptual level.

The theory is a conceptual explanation of a process that we have named 'demonstrating capability'. This means that the theory could be applied to other settings where people are concerned with demonstrating what they are capable of – that is, other settings involving assessment or appraisal (for example, workplaces). While each factor in each stage can be modified depending on the field of study being examined, the process will still operate. In this sense, the theory is modifiable: as time passes and conditions change, the theory should continue to fit, work and be relevant.

Conclusion

In this chapter we mapped the logistical aspects of advancing from the research problem to a grounded theory by explaining how an iterative approach to the study design was employed. This involved cycles of simultaneous data collection and analysis that informed the next round of data collection. The theory was developed from student data, which gives them a dominant 'voice' in the book. While we do not necessarily agree with all of the students' concerns, it means that we now have a comprehensive understanding of their perspectives on the fairness of assessment.

We now turn to the first of three chapters that explain the grounded theory 'demonstrating capability'.

Chapter 3

Sources of frustration with assessment

> Assessment acts as a mechanism to control students that is far more
> pervasive and insidious than most staff would be prepared to acknowledge.
>
> (Boud 1995: 35)

This is the first of three chapters in which we present the grounded theory
we have developed from a constant comparative process of data analysis.

In this chapter we describe the problem, as we have conceptualized it,
of the frustration undergraduate university students have with assessment.
We then introduce the concept of demonstrating capability – namely, that
students want opportunities to demonstrate their capability and have that
capability recognized. Such opportunity is provided through the process of
assessment, while recognition is provided by the marks given to a range
of assessment tasks. Students regard assessment as unfair if they perceive that
they have not been given the opportunity to demonstrate capability, or if
their capability has not been recognized. Thus, we introduce the substantive
theory of demonstrating capability: an explanation of students' perceptions
of the fairness of assessment, and their emotional and behavioural responses
to it.

Throughout these chapters we present a number of excerpts from
interviews with students. We think that the inclusion of the voices of the
students adds authenticity and veracity to the theory. Relevant extant
knowledge is also incorporated throughout the chapters. This knowledge is
drawn from a variety of disciplines including education, organizational
behaviour, organizational psychology and management studies, and helps to
embed the theory of demonstrating capability in wider theoretical bodies
of knowledge.

In this and subsequent chapters, academic staff, professors, assistant professors, lecturers, tutors or assessors will be referred to as teachers or teaching
staff. Occasionally it is necessary to refer to a teacher specifically as a tutor,
lecturer or course coordinator because of the context. 'Course' refers to the
individual subjects taught within a degree (for example, Mathematics 101).
'Programme' refers to the full degree (for example, Bachelor of Arts).

The problem of frustration with assessment

In grounded theory studies, researchers read, analyze and code data with the aim of identifying the central concerns of the group they are studying. This is an emergent process. As Jones and Noble note, 'the study problem will gradually emerge from the data as reflecting the main concern which the participants perceive they are confronting' (2007: 86).

The central problem we identified is that most students feel frustrated with their assessment experiences. They feel frustrated because they do not know and/or understand what their teachers expect them to do in assessment tasks, or what criteria and standards their teachers use to judge the quality of their performances.

For students to have a chance of success with an assessment item, they need to know and understand what their teachers expect them to do in assessment tasks. Course booklets are the main means of communicating teachers' expectations of assessment tasks in many universities. These are usually issued to students at the beginning of a course.

These course booklets are linked to assessment policy and procedure manuals, which could include a 'code of good practice'. Assessment policy and procedure manuals are available (usually online) to students for clarification about policy or procedural matters. Knowledge of the content of the assessment policy and procedure manual is essential for students wishing to challenge or question an assessment-related issue – at least if they wish to do so in an informed way. Interestingly, many students seem to be unaware of the existence of assessment policy and procedure manuals, with some thinking there is 'something somewhere' that they can refer to if they need help.

Assessment policy and procedures manuals are regularly revised and updated. They are important documents for teachers to consult when dealing with assessment matters. The manuals contain specific information that directs teachers to ensure students are well informed of assessment requirements. The information that teachers provide to students might include the following:

- advice about the criteria and standards by which performance is to be judged;
- the teachers' expectations of assessment tasks;
- the relationship of the assessment task to the programme's aims and objectives;
- the length requirements (word count);
- the weightings of different assessment tasks and their contribution towards the final grade;
- the form of presentation of the assessment task (essay, report, oral presentation, portfolio);

- submission dates, and criteria used to grant extensions and resubmissions;
- the content and skills to be assessed in examinations, and the nature of variations to standard requirements for examinations (for example, extra time, use of a language dictionary, use of a computer);
- the extent to which the assessment task(s) can be negotiated between the student and the teacher.

Sources of frustration

Unclear assessment criteria

Most contemporary universities recognize the need to communicate clear expectations about assessment to students undertaking their courses. At the University of South Australia, for example, a detailed 73-page *Assessment policies and procedures manual* (University of South Australia 2010) sets out the assessment parameters and the processes that are to be used in the case of disputes over assessment. Despite the directives in the manuals to make assessment criteria clear, students still find the expectations of teachers confusing. Students have differing opinions about what constitutes enough detail in course booklets, but all agree that clear assessment criteria are required, as illustrated by these comments:

> I think that people should be given the criteria of what you are being marked against. That would help everyone because you could then say this is what I followed.
>
> (Veronica)

> And certainly in terms of the lecturer or the examiner reinforcing why it is that they have chosen that particular grade, I think would actually assist them because they can say 'Well, hey, I marked what was there. This is the criteria; you failed. That's how I got the mark'. So it would actually be easier for the lecturer to explain the end mark as opposed to 'Oh, well, you know, Johnny did a really great job, you know, so much better than the last assignment', that type of thing.
>
> (Samantha)

Providing clear criteria enables students to examine the mark they receive against the criteria. Clear criteria also enable teachers to justify the marks they award if questioned by a student.

Our students had a number of suggestions to improve the content of course booklets. These included:

- specific guidelines that outline what is required to receive each of the possible grades in a marking scheme;

- examples of past assessment products, such as essays;
- lists of the concepts they are expected to apply;
- even how many references should be cited for each assessment piece.

Several of our students expressed concerns about unclear criteria. The first student refers to the grade 'P1'. This is from a system where grades awarded can be high distinction (HD, 85–100%), distinction (D, 75–84%), credit (C, 65–74%), pass level 1 (P1, 55–64%), pass level 2 (P2, 50–54%), fail level 1 (F1, 40–49%) or fail level 2 (F2, below 40%):

> It isn't fair that a booklet isn't detailed enough to at least show what is needed for a P1 or whatever.
>
> (Olive)

> With the assignments they give, case scenarios, you have to answer the questions but they don't have any dot points on what concepts to cover. I spoke to a number of people concerning that, and they're saying I have no idea what to write. I don't think that is fair at all.
>
> (Melanie)

> I don't know what is expected. I still haven't worked it out in the last couple of years. One of my major problems in doing an assignment is that I can't understand what they want exactly out of the assignment. It would be nice for them just to give an example of a past essay . . . It's not like you're going to copy it word for word because everyone's got it, but at least you've got a little bit of a ballpark, you know what roughly they want.
>
> (Nathan)

> A lot of people weren't very happy just because the lecturer didn't explain the assignment and didn't have a plan of what she wanted and yet when we went and approached her about it, she said 'you've got that freedom to do what you want' but she doesn't have a plan of what she wants in the course booklet, so you're not quite sure what she wants. So you do what you think she wants, take into account what she said in class, but then she says 'that's not really what I wanted'. You can't win!
>
> (Melanie)

When clarification is needed from teachers

If course booklets do not contain sufficient detail some students will approach teachers for more information. Several students discuss this:

> I think there's obviously some lecturers who give you a lot of guidance and a lot of criteria to cover and that's what they will mark it on and

you kind of come to expect that. And then there's others who, you know, don't give a lot of direction and therefore if you want a good mark you'll have to clarify what needs to go in it because really there's no direction or there's not a lot of direction, so it's up to you.

(Steve)

You're always told there is no need for you to write to the lecturer but, like I said before, that's not the way it is at all. You need to know what it is, look at what they want and you have to write to them. So you put yourself at a disadvantage if you don't go and actually find out.

(Veronica)

The person who has approached the lecturer has taken the initiative to do so because she has a problem. She was not exactly sure what the lecturer wanted so she has gone and approached the lecturer and clarified it. Whereas the other person has obviously thought, 'okay, I'll just go off and write it'. They haven't taken the initiative to go to the lecturer and I think that is fair, that the person who has put in more work, well really they have put in more work because they have gone and approached the lecturer and done what they wanted. I think that it is fair that they receive a higher mark.

(Melanie)

If you ask and you don't get the response that you require, then ask someone else and keep asking. And that's good business practice; that's what you do in the real world anyway. If someone asks you to do something out in the workforce and you don't know how to do it, you don't just sit there and go, 'I don't know how to do it'. You ask and you keep asking . . . Obviously you then get rewarded if you've gone that extra step.

(Samantha)

However, not all students are comfortable about approaching teachers to clarify assessment criteria. Darren says:

When you get a booklet or you get any information it is up to the student to ask for more or to do their own study because the amount of effort or research that you put in, that's the result you get. But I can't approach lecturers easily to ask questions. There is no less effort put in, the student who didn't ask. In my experience I don't talk to lecturers much about work and I wish I could but the longer it goes the harder it is . . . some people find other things harder than others, everyone finds something easier than others, and if it comes down to talking to your lecturers for more information some students can and others can't, and that can shape the mark at the end of it.

Darren's comment that 'some students can and others can't' talk to teachers is echoed in various ways by many other students. We found that high-achieving and/or mature age students are more confident in seeking clarification from teachers than younger students and/or lower achieving students.

Unlike Melanie, quoted above for believing that students seeking clarification from teachers deserve better marks, many students grapple with the fairness of having to ask for more information. They feel this potentially gives some students an advantage over others. As Tracy says:

> Both students were provided with the same information in their booklets. One of them has gone to the lecturer, off their own back, and has obviously got further clarification that she was going in the right direction – whereas the other one has read the booklet and made the assumption and hasn't got quite as good a mark. So I guess it is fair that the one who has got off her own back and done extra work probably deserves a better mark. But then on the other hand the booklet should provide enough information so that it is clear what the assessment is.

Another problem arises when teachers do not make themselves available to students to clarify assessment criteria. Melanie explains:

> In course X, all they have is the question and you are not allowed to go and ask the lecturer at all about anything, not even to do with the assignment, because there are so many people in the course they don't allow students to do that. And the question you could answer any way you like and you just think 'what am I supposed to write?' It is hard to know what they want. I think that is unfair that you can't actually approach them.

The general view of students is that it is unfair if teachers do not make themselves available for consultation, although some students consider that 'they are all being treated the same'. In these cases they do not say it is totally unfair, even if they do not agree with or like the stance.

Not understanding a mark

Some of the frustration of students is alleviated when they understand why they receive a particular mark for an assessment task. However, often students do not understand the marks they receive, and their frustration continues. This is illustrated by Pip and Tracy:

> I actually completed an assignment in first semester and a very similar assignment in second semester and the mark was a P1 to a distinction

and I couldn't work that out. Very similar quality work. Just a different course but the same teacher.

(Pip)

I've had ones back that have been surprisingly good so I guess I have trouble weighing up what I did different in that one to the one I did when I just passed. I guess pinpointing that is the trouble I'm having.

(Tracy)

Travis provides another example. He was awarded a P1 for an assignment. He questioned the teacher to ascertain what his errors were, as he wanted to improve his marks with his next assignment. Travis thought he had taken the feedback into account, but in the next assignment he got a lower mark, a P2. This frustrated him so much that he decided to 'take the pressure off himself': 'I just gave up putting in extra effort and, just like I said, thrashed it around with other students and said – I'll be buggered if I'm going to, you know, go the extra mile.' Travis put in less effort with the final two assessment pieces and for these he received credits – higher marks than the previous two assignments. This experience left him completely confused about assessment in that course with that teacher.

Nearly all students want to understand why they receive a particular mark. Samantha, a high-achieving student, received two reports back from a teacher and felt that they were ranked in the wrong order. She felt that the report that received a higher mark should have been lower and vice versa. Samantha wanted to understand why the reports received the marks they did:

... the fact that I couldn't understand why one report was marked lower than expected. Why or where it was and certainly there wasn't enough commentary for me to be able to say, 'oh, yeah, right, yeah I missed that' ... I actually thought that they should have been reversed with the lower report marked higher and the higher one lower, and that's actually what I said to the lecturer. I said, 'look, I know that this means nothing to you because at the end of the day my overall grade for those two reports won't change but I actually think they should be reversed'. So no, I wasn't suggesting for one minute that the other one should be put up, to be equal to the other high one, no.

(Samantha)

What concerned Samantha was that she did not understand the teacher's logic in assigning the two grades. Many high-achieving students comment that they want to know where they lose marks, even if they receive a high distinction. If teachers cannot justify the marks they award, students are unsure what they need to do to improve, or to retain their grade, in future assignments.

The frustration students experience in not knowing and/or understanding what their teachers expect them to do in assessment tasks are often related to two very specific, tangible issues: word counts and deadlines.

Word count confusion

Word counts cause frustration for students in three ways. First, they are frustrated if they do not know what is meant by a word count – that is, how words are counted and what words are included in the count (for example, reference list, footnotes, appendices). Second, they are frustrated if they do not know whether the teacher expects them to adhere strictly to the word count. Third, they become frustrated if they do not know the consequences of presenting work that is under or over the required word count.

Most of the students we interviewed assumed that teachers expect the computer-generated word count to be the guide of how much to write. Yet in speaking with a random group of 12 colleagues, we found that most of these teachers estimated the word count of assignments by the number of pages and some did not count at all, despite stating a word count for assessment items in their course booklets. Such inconsistency inevitably leads to greater student frustration.

We found that a small number of teachers still count the average number of words in a line excluding small words of three letters or less. This practice was the standard way of conducting word counts before word processing programs became commonplace in the late 1990s. The difference between the two totals is substantial; the computer-generated system gives a word total approximately 1.44 times greater than that of the manual counting system, so an assignment with a computer word count of 3,600 words will be manually counted as 2,500.

Even a simple, apparently clear, statement in a course booklet such as 'the computer-generated word count must be included at the end of the submitted assignment' can still cause frustration. Students do not know if that means they need to include words that are headings and numbers, abstracts, appendices, reference lists, in-text references, captions for figures and illustrations and tables, or direct quotes.

Whether teachers expect the word count to be adhered to is of great concern to students who exceed it, as they do not know if they will be penalized. Some teachers accept a deviation of plus or minus 10 per cent of the stated word count but do not necessarily state this in course booklets. Students find it intensely frustrating when there are no consequences for students who exceed the word count, particularly if they had worked hard to adhere to the stated word count.

Students cite various actions by teachers if an assignment exceeds the word count. These actions range from a line being drawn across the page at the point where the teacher deems the word count has been met and refusing to read after that point, to not penalizing at all for an excessive word count. Polly reported once being advantaged by exceeding a word count: '. . . the 4,000-word report we had last year for lecturer Z, mine was 8,000 and a lot of other people's were about the same and people who wrote more actually got higher grades.'

Ginny mentions a very similar example where a student was upset when she reportedly adhered to the word count and another student did not:

> Although the university policy is that 10 per cent either way is acceptable – that's a policy that's been in a number of courses, but then I think I've only ever seen one lecturer who has actually adhered to it. This morning, for the tenth time, one of the students had a whinge to me about how she did an essay that was 2,000 words, which was the stipulated amount, someone else did one that was 8,000 and got a high distinction and she [the whinging student] got a distinction and she wasn't happy. It really bugs her, because this is 18 months ago that this happened and she's still talking about it . . . The comments that the person who received the distinction got were, 'You should have expanded on this particular issue' and, yes, she wasn't happy about that.
>
> (Ginny)

Most students are not concerned that teachers have varied expectations of word counts. They try hard to accommodate them. However, they become very frustrated when they do not know what the expectations are, and when teachers do not apply their own word count guidelines.

Deadlines

Another area that causes much frustration for students is the deadline, or due date and time, for submission of assessment tasks. Similar to the issues with word counts, students report that teachers have differing understandings of deadlines. Teachers are also inconsistent in their expectations of whether students adhere to the stated deadlines. Furthermore, teachers do not always articulate the consequences of submitting an assessment task late.

Students also have various interpretations of what constitutes a due date and time. Ursula is very definite about the importance of submitting her work on time: 'I think that time, that deadlines should be strict and afterwards you do lose marks and people should be made aware of that.'

Other students cannot see an issue with assignments not meeting the deadline. Melanie provides an example of a more flexible approach:

> I think you should have a leeway of probably an hour or probably half an hour, for lecturers to have that time, to say to the students it is due

at four o'clock so they know to hand it up but if someone hands it up at ten past four I think that is fair to take it and not deduct 10 per cent because it is not an extra day that they have actually spent on it.

Students are aware of differences between teachers' enforcement of deadlines. Tracy gives the example of a teacher saying to a class on a Friday, the day an essay was due, that they could submit their work on the following Monday, because 'I don't intend to mark them until next week'. When we mentioned this example to other students in interviews, their responses were incredibly mixed. Some students were irate that this could happen, whereas others felt it was fair and reasonable.

Melanie is concerned that handing an assignment in slightly after the deadline may result in work not being assessed:

I've spoken to people in other courses and people who have handed up assignments five minutes late haven't been marked at all. The lecturer just hasn't marked them, given them back with no grade, so hasn't marked them. They've failed them on it. With 'course D', one of my friends said people handed them up five minutes late, it was an optional assignment, you had the choice to do it or not, and the lecturer just didn't include it. If they'd put in all that work then fair enough if it was late they could have got a 10 per cent deduction but not to mark it at all is really unfair.

All of the students we interviewed feel it is grossly unfair not to assess an overdue assignment. If teachers plan not to mark assignments handed in after the stated time, students want to know this. They also say that if they knew the logic behind the decision it would help them understand the teachers' actions. Students, while not necessarily agreeing with this approach, are less frustrated if they understand the rationale for the decision.

As with word counts, students are not particularly concerned about teachers varying their interpretation of a deadline; their greater concern is not knowing what their teachers mean by a deadline. In particular, they want to know if deadlines will be adhered to, and what consequences will follow from not meeting set deadlines.

All of the students we spoke to report feeling frustrated about some aspect of their assessment at university. However, there are significant differences between students in their levels of frustration, the effects on their well-being, and what they chose to do about their frustration.

The next section outlines the basic social process of demonstrating capability. Students engage in this process to address their feelings of frustration with assessment.

Demonstrating capability

Students want the opportunity to demonstrate their capability and have that capability recognized. This was apparent throughout the interviews, with students often referring to 'having the chance to demonstrate what I am capable of'.

The need to demonstrate capability is implicit in many comments the students make about the fairness of assessment. As several students explain:

> There should be a balance of work, to tie up theory in practical situations and that having major marks on something doesn't really reflect the student capabilities. Having an even spread of work can show how well they do, and that's fair.
>
> (Melanie)

> It's better to spread it over a number of things. Some people won't do well at some things, people won't understand or whatever, like that. It just comes easier if you have a range of things.
>
> (Duncan)

> As long as they get your potential out of you. As long as they get what they need to prove to them that you can actually do it.
>
> (Nathan)

> What would be the fairest way for you to get the best marks you can by showing me that you have got the knowledge?
>
> (Veronica)

> Exams aren't fair for the students who have trouble with them because they don't get to show what they are capable of.
>
> (Darren)

Opportunity to demonstrate capability

If students perceive that they have the opportunity to demonstrate capability, they view assessment as fair. Students view the opportunity to demonstrate capability as a process involving many interrelated actions. This process begins when they are given an assessment task, and continues until they submit. To have the opportunity to demonstrate capability, students need to understand what their teachers expect them to do in assessment tasks. Students consider that having the opportunity to demonstrate capability involves many other things too, including the perceived relevance of assessment items, the availability of teachers, the operation of procedures to request extensions, the ability of teachers to communicate with students, and the way they are treated by teachers.

Whether capability has been recognized

Students judge whether capability has been recognized by the mark they receive for an assessment item. If students perceive that their capability has not been recognized (for example, having received a grade lower than expected), they view assessment as unfair. In deciding if their capability has been recognized, students take into account the level of access they had to their teachers, and the nature and quality of the feedback they have received from their teachers, among other things. The grade is important to students when they make a fairness judgment; they are applying distributive justice principles. In addition to the grade, students apply procedural justice principles (for example, the receipt of feedback) and interpersonal justice principles (for example, treatment by teachers when interacting with students).

Conclusion

Students have varied understandings of what it means to be able to demonstrate capability, or what capabilities are being assessed. Understanding this point is critical to understanding why some students regard something as fair, yet others regard the same thing as unfair. Students have varied expectations. For example, some students believe that it is important to meet deadlines because for them it shows their time management and organizational skills, while others believe that it is more important to show they have the ability to analyse concepts and apply them in a written piece of work. Each of these students might have a different view on the fairness of receiving a deduction for late submission of work.

If students do not know, or do not understand, what is expected of them in assessment tasks, then they need strategies to help them deal with their frustration. For example, finding out what teachers actually want in assessment tasks is likely to reduce the level of frustration experienced by students.

Having explained what causes this frustration and having introduced the concept of demonstrating capability we now introduce the theory itself. The theory explains how a student identifies whether an assessment is unfair, and how they attempt to resolve the problem of frustration related to assessment. By identifying and explaining the process, the theory of demonstrating capability provides an explanation of students' perceptions of the fairness of assessment, and the resultant behaviour.

The substantive theory of demonstrating capability has two stages. Stage one, which is explained in the next chapter, is the 'deciding fairness' stage. Here, students make their fairness judgments when talking with others, and comparing their work with their previous work and the work of others. In making these comparisons, effort is the major criterion students use to judge whether the outcome of assessment matches their input. Students also make comparisons with personal expectations and past experiences, taking into account six key considerations when deciding if an assessment is fair.

Stage two of the theory is 'responding' to perceptions of unfairness and is explained in detail in Chapter 5. This stage captures students' emotional reactions to a judgment of unfairness, and their responses to their judgments.

Chapter 4

Deciding the fairness
of assessment

Teacher: How many diamonds have you got?
Student: I don't have any diamonds.
Teacher: Then you fail!
Student: But you didn't ask me about my jade.

(Biggs 2003: 160)

In the previous chapter we explained that the main concern of students about assessment is frustration because they do not know and/or understand what their teachers expect them to do in assessment tasks, or what criteria and standards are applied by their teachers to judge the quality of their performances. We also introduced the idea that students regard assessment as fair if the process allows them an opportunity to demonstrate capability, and if the product, in the form of a mark or grade, indicates that their capability has been recognized. Furthermore, students have varying perceptions about what demonstrating capability means, and what is involved in demonstrating capability.

In this chapter we describe the first stage of the basic social process of demonstrating capability. This is the stage we call 'deciding fairness', and it is illustrated in the top half of Figure 4.1.

Most students only review the details of the assessment task when they receive an unexpected grade or mark. The grade or mark triggers a reflective process that involves re-evaluating whether they had sufficient opportunities to demonstrate their capabilities. The mark itself also promotes reflection about:

- past assessment performances
- others' performances
- effort
- personal expectations and past experiences.

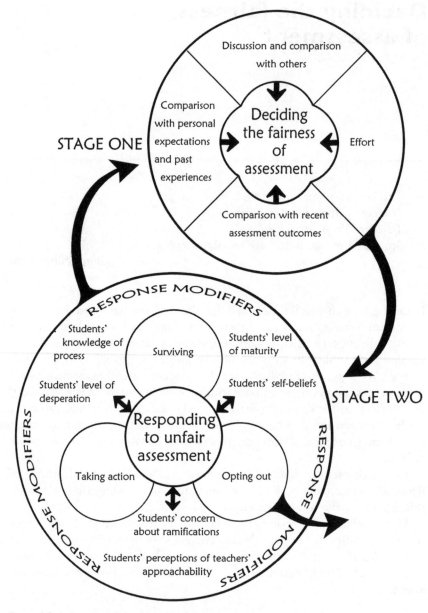

Figure 4.1 A diagram of the process of demonstrating capability

Comparison with recent assessment outcomes

When students receive a mark for an assessment item they make a judgment of fairness. As well as comparing effort, which will be discussed later, students reflect on other experiences of assessment and often compare a mark with those they have received in other courses. Students take into account the feedback from their teachers – if they can understand it, and if there is enough – and some students will crosscheck the feedback against the criteria of the assessment item.

Most students are confident that they know the standard of their work. When a mark is too different from those they usually receive, or from those they expect to achieve, they identify that something is 'wrong'. They are applying procedural justice principles. Louise explains her thinking:

> I mean I had other assignments and I expected that I'd get 17 out of 20 and got 13 . . . I know the standard of work that I hand in and what I had across the board handed in and my level of work is generally at that level, certainly not – I don't get a P1 or a credit . . . for my work; I normally get distinctions for my work. And when I don't, then there's something wrong.

The benchmark for what a student expects to receive in assessment is often determined by earlier marks in a course. As Alise explains: 'The appreciation of the mark you have, really depends on the marks you've got before because if you start with a really good mark you are tending to not let yourself go lower.' The expectation is modified over time depending on subsequent marks, but most students report having a general understanding of the mark they should receive.

The first marks or grades in a course or programme are important in setting a benchmark and giving students' confidence that they understand the expectations of the course and the teacher. However, for students beginning university for the first time, knowing what is expected of them can be problematic. For example, Alise, a student on an international exchange, talks about having to adjust to new expectations:

> I think the first mark is the most important, especially when you change environments [moving from a French to an Australian university] because if your first mark in any course is a good mark this is really encouraging and it makes you feel you understood what they are expecting from me so I am going to follow this way, whereas if you had [a] bad mark in the beginning, you don't give up but you just say 'this will never work', it is stupid but it happens.

Similarly, school leavers entering university for the first time may be very disappointed if their first assessment grades do not meet their school-related expectations.

Initially, then, students draw on their relatively recent assessment experiences to make judgments about the fairness of the assessment process and outcome. Later they engage in more detailed comparisons with other students.

Discussion and comparison with others

After a preliminary consideration of their grade, most students talk with other students and compare their marks. It seems much of this talk is for 'sense-making purposes'. This is a term used by Sias and Jablin who found that co-workers often discuss differential treatment, which suggests 'that evaluations regarding the fairness of differential treatment are often socially constructed by co-workers through communication' (1995: 30). Perceptions of fairness influence discourse and co-workers are far more likely to talk about differential treatment they regard as unfair. Sias and Jablin suggest that this discourse influences fairness perceptions and is not just to complain or vent frustration.

It is common for students to talk and compare their assessment outcomes with others. Some students discuss their mark with several students; others report talking with only one or two. Most students compare their marks with those in their friendship group, or immediate circle of friends. The discussion widens beyond the usual circle if something is perceived to be particularly unfair. Several students explain how they compare their experiences with friends and peers:

> Mmm. I guess find out what other people are doing, if there is anything you can compare it to, any other situations, courses, or lecturers, talk to other people and find out what else is going on . . . Amongst friends . . . 'oh what did you get for that?' Or when assignments are returned people do, probably more in the friendship circles but definitely do it with the other people, you usually know who did the best. It's easy to find out.
>
> (Laura)

> Umm, I probably discuss it first with my peers and say 'look, you know, what do you think about this incident? Do you think that that is fair or what do you interpret by that?'
>
> (Tracy)

> Pretty much actually, you find out during the year – you know your friends' work, you know what they are good at, you know how they work, you know what they read – you know how they pass their work and stuff, how they treat stuff and how they write, there's always, people you can tell, look, you get a distinction, or a high distinction.
>
> (Tom)

We've just always compared, since day one, especially the first assignment we all got back from lecturer X. Unless you've got something to compare against you don't know what is fair/unfair. If you can't compare you would just assume a low grade means you need to improve.

(Polly)

Receiving a particular grade is not the only trigger that leads students to make judgments of fairness. The judgment may also be influenced by comparisons with the marks of other students. Olive explains:

You tend to talk to people, and if that's the way he or she has marked the assignment, and so I guess then you'd say that's the level . . . but if I started getting P1s or P2s for something that I at least thought was worth a credit or a distinction then I might [think it is unfair]. As I said, it depends on what the marking is; if everyone else is getting P1s and credits, well that is probably what the level of it was.

Ursula describes a similar process of comparing her results with others:

If I got a P2 [low pass] for something and my pal that I'm normally pretty [equal with] . . . came up with a distinction, then I would definitely be questioning it, but because I average credits and distinctions anyway, I would [question it] if friends I sit with came back and got HDs, and some of them are at my level, or below and got above me, then I might question it, if they got HDs and I'd come out with P1s.

Some students receiving a lower mark than they expect will talk with other students to determine the standard of marking. This suggests that students construct different levels of fairness. They consider it to be 'more fair' to get a low mark if members of their reference group achieve similar marks. This process of constant comparison is also consistent with equity theory: people compare themselves to others by focusing on whether the ratio of their inputs to outcomes is equal to the input–outcome ratio of the others (Adams 1965). Students often compare their own input and outcome for an assessment piece with others in their class, or even other people they know who study in another university. As Greenberg (2005) explains, it is important to understand that equity theory does not necessarily deal with objective standards; it deals with inputs and outcomes as they are perceived by people.

Talking about and comparing marks with others is not only used to make fairness judgments, but also to understand what is required of an assessment item. Some students even go as far as reading others' assignments to benchmark their own performances. In particular, viewing the work of high-achieving students helps students to understand what is needed to achieve higher marks. This strategy could be utilized more effectively by teachers. Samantha speaks about other students asking to see her work:

I've had people come up to me and have asked to see my work, compared theirs to it and I don't have a problem with that . . . I see that as part of information sharing . . . I actually think it's good practice when you're at university. I mean I see that as one of the big bonuses of coming to university, is that sharing of information . . . feedback, I think the feedback aspect – if you can see that the person that got the good grade has got much better tables than you, better graphics, the layout is better, their content is far superior than yours, you can pick up on that and go, 'oh, next time I'm going to do that and then I might get the high distinction that I'm after'. So I don't see that as a bad thing.

While discussing and comparing marks with others is commonplace and important for students in making fairness judgments, it can also be problematic for two key reasons. First, it is difficult for students to make accurate comparisons when assessment tasks involve high levels of subjective judgment. Second, many students admit that they are not honest when talking with peers, particularly friends, who tend to be the ones with whom they share things. Students often make erroneous fairness judgments because they are influenced by social expectations to maintain harmonious relationships. David speaks about the time a friend of his asked his opinion about the low mark he got for an essay:

Last year one of my mates asked me to look at his essay. I wasn't going to tell him it was shit, excuse my language, because how would it look to be telling your friend you don't think his work is any good?

Given these insights into students' thinking, teachers could incorporate activities that enable students to explore the interpersonal dimension of forming views about the fairness of assessment. This could assist students to become more attuned to multiple perspectives on issues to do with assessment.

Not all fairness judgments are flawed, however, as the following example from Nadia suggests that comparisons made with others can be accurate. In this case, Nadia had received a distinction for an assignment and thought it unfair; having sustained a high level of effort over a number of weeks and invested a lot of time and energy into the work, she had expected a high distinction. Nadia was very upset about the way it was marked: the 'vague comments, ticks here and there that meant you could tell it wasn't read, he hadn't looked at it properly'. She then compared her work with three other students who had also received distinctions. This confirmed for her that the teacher had not paid sufficient attention to any of the pieces of work. For example, one student had accidentally handed in a draft version (which included square brackets throughout, with the words 'insert word here'), and this was not commented upon. The other students also had random ticks and vague comments. Two of the students had worked on their assignments the day before and failed to make obvious editorial changes. Following her examination of the other students' work, Nadia felt that her work was of a higher quality. She was also outraged because of the comparative amount of effort she had put in, and the obvious failure of the teacher to distinguish between the various pieces of work.

Effort

In addition to making comparisons with their recent assessment outcomes, and discussing and making comparisons with the marks of other students, students consider effort when making fairness judgments.

Success is frequently perceived to be the result of hard work, and indeed the effort put into something often influences the outcome. Early in their school education, students often receive feedback on effort, for example: 'good effort', 'needs more effort', 'with more effort your work would achieve a higher grade' – and thus learn that effort brings reward. Students' expectations of an outcome are therefore heavily predicated on their perception of how much effort they have put in. As several students reveal, the link between effort, outcome and a perception of fairness is strong:

> I generally know what it is going to be. If I know I've put the effort in, it's going to be decent; if I haven't, it's not going to be worth it.
>
> (Duncan)

> I guess it [fairness] stands for possibly being rewarded for what you have done, the effort you put into something, possibly you see it back in grades.
>
> (Laura)

> If you don't put in a good effort there is no point expecting [a higher grade]. You get what you deserve.
>
> (Victor)

It is clear that these and other students are applying a key tenet of basic equity theory (Adams 1963, 1965), in which the extent of congruence between expected and actual outcome is an important element in the judgment of fairness. It is not the receipt of a low grade that students believe to be unfair, but a grade that is lower than expected (Tata 1999). Most students apply a measure of effort to predict what grade they will receive.

When students perceive some congruence between effort and outcome they are generally content, but when the two do not match, students tend to feel confused, demoralized and unhappy, which often leads them to question the fairness of the mark. As several students explain:

> A lot of students sort of laugh about it, 'I did that last night and I got a P1', then they spend weeks on it, put a lot of time into it and still get a P1.
>
> (Darren)

> And I went, 'Hang on, I mean I put almost as much work into it as I did with the other one, what's the go here?'
>
> (Ian)

> I remember putting a lot of effort into some of those assignments and when I got to the end I only just got a P1 or something.
>
> (Nathan)

Students not only use effort to gauge the grade they believe they deserve; they also make crude or rough judgments about the comparative effort of others. As Melanie and Travis explain, students frequently base their estimates on their knowledge of other students' work habits and lifestyle:

> You figure out how much work each person has put in.
>
> (Melanie)

> You are always sort of wondering how other people are doing because you know a lot of the times how much effort they're putting in as well. You never know exactly how much they're putting in but you can [tell] – just from what they say and do as well.
>
> (Travis)

Darren is one of the few students who recognize that effort can be misspent:

> [Students] think the amount of effort they put in should then translate to a mark . . . If a student does not believe they are getting out what they put in, it is not fair. This is judged by time, effort, energy, hours of sleep, books read, social hours, etc. Sometimes time and energy can be misspent. Then it is a misunderstanding that creates a feeling of unfairness.

Students often fail, at least initially, to take into account whether they met the requirements of the assessment task and if their efforts were well directed.

Many students believe that their effort should count towards the final grade. Adams (2005) shows that students consistently believe effort should contribute to significantly more of a final course grade than do their teachers. He found that more than 70 per cent of students expect to receive at least a C, in a range from A to F, when they work hard in courses that are not part of their major – even when they fail to show in their assessment that they have learned the minimum amount of information that the assessment task was intended to test.

Many students feel 'hard done by' when they invest significant effort and receive a lower mark than others *who they perceive as putting in less effort.* This kind of thinking is based on principles of distributive justice. As Nathan suggests, this can influence students' levels of satisfaction with their assigned mark: 'I talked to some people and I couldn't understand why they got a better mark than I did and, yeah, [they] didn't put as much effort into it.'

So, what do students mean by effort? Students speak about effort in diverse and usually very general ways, often interchanging the words 'effort' with 'time' and 'work'. Most often *time* is equated with effort; the students believe that spending a lot of time on an assignment or task constitutes a significant effort. Varying benchmarks are used to define effort in completing an assignment; while one student refers to a sustained input of time over two or three weeks, another means giving up a Saturday night's entertainment. These varied benchmarks mean that comparisons of effort to make judgments of fairness about other students' marks is problematic, particularly given the different abilities and experiences students bring to tasks, and the varied study habits they employ.

It seems reasonable, however, for a student to use their perception of their own effort to make comparisons between their grades within and across courses. If students expend a certain amount of effort in one assignment and receive a grade that is vastly different from that of another assignment for which they expended equal effort, it is perhaps logical that they look for other explanations for the different result.

The notion of equating time with effort is not new. There have been very few studies of the relationship between study effort and academic performance, but each has used time as a sole, or major, factor in quantifying effort. A series of studies spanning 12 years at the University of Michigan by Schuman *et al.* (1985) repeatedly found no significant correlation between hours studied and grades. The findings of a study by Michaels and Miethe (1989) suggested that the relationship between effort and reward is mediated by several factors. Class attendance and time spent studying are associated with higher grades for those who study throughout the week, but not for students who study intensively just before an exam or when an assignment is due. Interestingly, study time significantly improved the grades achieved by students in the early years of their university programme but did not affect outcomes for students in their final years. Otherwise, Michaels and Miethe's results were similar to those of Schuman and colleagues. Killen (1994), using time as a measure of effort, found that students, on average, expected to spend just over half the time studying that their teachers expected them to spend – about 15 hours per week instead of about 25 hours per week.

Using time to represent effort is probably common because there are numerous problems with attempting to quantify academic effort (Rau and

Durand 2000). These problems relate to: how to define the quality of effort; oversimplification of students' study patterns; the connection between ability and effort; the effect of other students' leisure activities, which may undermine their focus during study time; the fact that the number of hours of study are only a measure of present efforts and do not consider the relationship of years of past effort, and so on. These problematic factors are frequently not taken into account by students when linking effort to time spent on task.

Some students assume that a good mark is based on expending a lot of effort. This assumption is challenged when they perceive that their peers apply less effort but still achieve a higher grade. An example is a student who thinks that it is unfair when someone can get good marks in a course after studying the day before an exam, yet receive the same mark overall as a student who sustains an effort studying throughout the semester. This student feels that effort should be exerted to warrant a reward (good mark), and studying for a short period of time does not constitute applying effort.

As noted above, students make direct comparisons between the effort they expend on an assignment (often linked to the time they spend working on the assignment) and the grade or mark they expect. If students make a significant effort and their marks are lower than they expect, their initial reaction is often that it is unfair, particularly if they believe that they met the criteria of the assessment task. On the other hand, if they put in a limited amount of effort and get a grade that is higher than they expect, they view it as good luck. Students laugh at the idea of asking a teacher to lower their grade. As one student said, 'It is just like when you get extra change in a shop. You're not going to give it back are you?'

A few students comment on their effort, not only in terms of time they spend on a task, but also in relation to the amount of contact that they initiate with teachers before an assignment is due. Many, such as Melanie, view approaching a teacher as expending effort that will result in getting a better mark: '[I] think that is fair, that the person who has put in more work, well really they have put in more work because they have gone and approached the lecturer and done what they wanted.' However, other students are unsure if this is just. They cite, among other potential factors, work commitments, part-time status, home commitments, lack of confidence and nervousness as reasons why some people are unable to consult with teachers about assignments. This shows that students apply procedural, interpersonal and informational justice elements to their judgment of fairness. Students are unsure whether they receive the same amount of information, they worry whether the teacher will be approachable and they feel that they do not have the same opportunities due to other life commitments.

It appears that students who only equate effort with time spent on an assignment are perhaps less able to use effort as an accurate measure of fairness than those students who recognize that quality of time spent on a task (perhaps including consulting with a teacher) is more important than the number of hours. Given these insights into students' thinking about effort, teachers could engage students in conversations about their perceptions of effort. This could assist students to become more discerning in their use of effort in making judgments about the fairness of a grade. This would also make explicit the broad range of students' understandings about this issue.

In summary, perception of effort is a key factor affecting students' judgments about the relative fairness of assessment. Students generally expect there to be a strong connection between the effort they expend on an assessment item, and the outcome in the form of a grade. This is at times problematic, as students have varied understandings about what constitutes effort and do not always take into account the quality of their effort and whether they understand the criteria of an assessment task.

Comparison with personal expectations and past experiences

The grade or mark that a student receives is an important component in their judgment of fairness of assessment. However, students make each fairness judgment in context, taking into account up to six key considerations. They do not necessarily attribute the same level of significance to each consideration. These considerations influence how students perceive their chance to demonstrate capability.

Students are strongly influenced by their past experiences. For example, Louise, a final-year honours student, speaks of how her expectation of contact with teaching staff was formed by her experience in an undergraduate degree at another university:

> It's completely different here than to university Y. At university Y you never saw your lecturer, they didn't actually know your name, where here they actually know who you are and speak to you. At university Y they never actually spoke to you, they lectured at you and they went off to their office and that was the last you saw of them. I don't know, some people I suppose it does, [but] for me it doesn't bother me because I haven't needed that access to lecturers but if you have issues then I suppose it does come up – and it's probably because I've never had access to the lecturers at university Y and that was my grounding at university – you just didn't.

Louise acknowledges that her current expectation of staff contact is lower than her peers who, having completed their undergraduate degrees in the same university at which they were completing honours, have come to expect more contact with lecturers.

The following comment by Nadine, a mature age student, shows how past experience of being concerned about 'gaining a reputation' influences her current expectations, and how the encouragement of a lecturer made a difference to her confidence about asking questions:

> ... the minute you stand out as being something that's a trouble maker or anything that's different you will be victimized as I saw in my previous workplace in the armed services. From that, coming here you are still in that train of thought that 'okay, I'm not going to rock the boat because this will happen to me'. But I think once you get into an environment and it is constantly pushed at you about equity and you start to believe it then you take action. So whereas last year I was very much influenced by my previous work [as an employee], this year I've moved out of it a bit because people like [lecturer X] who are constantly talking about equity and who very much have an open-door policy – I'd be much more confident to actually say 'look I'm not too comfortable about this assessment'.

As Nadine's comments show, what is considered important does not necessarily remain static throughout the life of a student. As students learn more about the university system – progressing through to higher year levels, accruing and analysing feedback from a growing stock of submitted assignments, and from working with others in groups – their expectations begin to change, as do the factors that influence their judgments about the fairness of assessment.

There are six key considerations, related to personal expectations and past experiences, that students take into account when making fairness judgments about assessment:

- whether there is a 'level playing field';
- the nature and extent of feedback about their assessment;
- the balance and variety of assessment tasks;
- the relevance of assessment tasks;
- whether the teachers are skilful;
- whether the teachers display a caring attitude.

The ensuing discussion of these six considerations is necessarily quite lengthy. While the considerations are presented as separate entities, there is a degree of interconnectedness among them. The six considerations are illustrated in Figure 4.2.

Level playing field

One consideration students take into account when deciding if assessment is fair is whether they are operating on a 'level playing field'. This term comes from the natural language used by students:

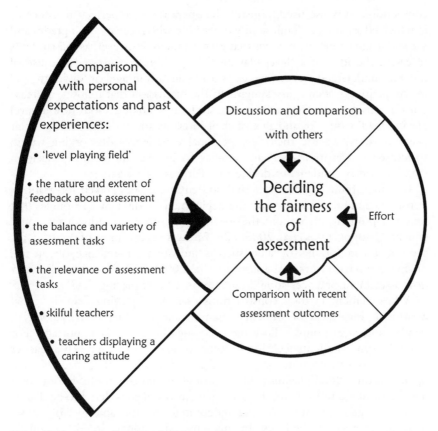

Figure 4.2 Stage one: Deciding the fairness of assessment

If students had been given the same information it would have been much fairer, because everyone would have been on the same level playing field.

(Ginny)

Students' idea of fairness is having the perceived same opportunities as other students. As long as they are presented with a level playing field . . .

(Darren)

In everyday usage, the sporting metaphor of playing on a 'level playing field' refers to any competition in which 'players' compete with each other 'equally' without having any 'unfair' advantages or disadvantages. The term is used in economics to describe the most desirable conditions for 'free market' competition. It is also used to justify the operation of a 'perfect' meritocracy in which effort and academic ability determine who receives good grades and the social and economic rewards that go with them. However, as our students revealed, the idea of a 'level playing field' is highly contested because of different understandings of what constitutes an 'advantage' or 'disadvantage' in competitive academic assessment. In the discussion that follows, we tease out the tensions and contradictions in students' thinking about how a 'level playing field' works for and against their interests and those of some of their peers. That is, we use their very personal experiences of working within structured university assessment regimes to unravel the complex decision making used by students to decide the 'fairness' of assessment.

It is important to point out that students' everyday, taken-for-granted, 'sense-making practices' involve 'the deployment of discursive resources that function primarily to uphold the ideals of meritocracy, individualism and equality' (Augoustinos *et al.* 2005: 336–7). As we show, most of our students promote the importance of values such as 'individual self–reliance, obedience, discipline and hard work' (Augoustinos *et al.* 2005: 317) when they talk about how assessment practices should operate on a 'level playing field'.

A key element in their constructions of a 'level playing field' is 'equal treatment' regardless of students' membership of different social, racial, gender and age groups. 'Treating everyone the same' is important. For example, some students feel that if no one is allowed to approach a teacher about an assessment item, or get feedback on a draft copy, then they are operating on a 'level playing field'. Although potentially useful information may be withheld from them, this arrangement is still considered to be 'fairer' than individual students receiving different forms and amounts of assessment information or feedback. In this sense, all students are either equally advantaged or equally disadvantaged.

While most students subscribe to this 'equal treatment' position, some challenge the simplicity of crass meritocratic ideals that ignore the operation of historic and systemic factors that advantage some groups (e.g. white, middle-class, able-bodied, heterosexual, male) and disadvantage others (Indigenous, poor, disabled, same-sex-attracted, female). For example, some students disagree about which individual circumstances should be taken into account in granting extra time in exams. They question whether students who are disadvantaged in some way deserve to be compensated to enable them to operate on a 'level playing field'. These students feel that 'affirmative action' is appropriate, as illustrated here:

> It probably is fair in a way – those people [non-English speaking background, Aboriginal and Torres Strait Islander] have . . . some sort of disadvantage and for them to do as well as everyone else they sometimes need that extra help. I think it is pretty fair really.
>
> (Duncan)

I think that is fair because it's not her first language so she hasn't honestly been brought up on English; she's had to learn it herself. I think that is fair, definitely, because you'd expect that in another country yourself as well, if you were in another country. It is very hard to speak another language.

(Melanie)

Student X I think should have extra time, like she is visually impaired. I think that's fine; I have no problems with that at all.

(Olive)

Interestingly, these sentiments don't seem to apply in all situations involving racial differences. Olive, although believing that students with a visual impairment should receive extra time in exams, has issues with Indigenous students receiving the same:

I guess if they're not English-speaking and they're doing the same exam as you then they need a bit of extra assistance but, um, I guess in terms of people like Aboriginals and things like that then in some ways that is a bit unfair because they're the same sort of people as we are in a sense . . . if they're just growing up here or whatever then they shouldn't have any extra but then that's the way that Australia is with those sorts of people; that sounds a terrible way of putting it . . . it depends on what sort of background they've come from . . . if they're just growing up like me in a normal sort of household, family, whatever and they're going to uni along with me then I don't see why [they should receive extra assistance].

Olive constructs affirmative action as 'undermining meritocratic ideals that [reward] individuals on their merit and proven ability. Meritocratic ideals [are] presented as "consensual" values that [are] central to a fair and just society that treats everyone equally' (Augoustino *et al.* 2005: 319). Similarly, Tom, who has recently migrated to Australia and is eligible for extra time in exams because English is not his first language, thinks the policy is apt but not something he chooses to use because it would shield him from the rigours of meritocratic competition. Tom believes that to compete in the 'real' world for a job he needs to be judged in the same way as everyone else, and if he gets through university using extra time in exams he might find himself unable to cope once he begins work.

At the heart of these contradictory views of what constitutes a 'level playing field' are different beliefs about whether a pre-existing advantage or disadvantage should 'count' in the competition for good grades. For some students:

. . . equality was largely defined in terms of treating everyone the same regardless of social category membership. In these accounts, social groups were stripped of their historical and social location in society and were positioned as equivalent and interchangeable.

(Augoustinos *et al.* 2005: 318)

In other words, 'being different' from the majority group was not accepted by some students as a reason to justify the abandonment of 'equal treatment' principles. For others, pre-existing 'disadvantages' became the focus of compensatory actions designed to make the assessment 'game' fairer and more equitable. Given these insights into students' thinking about what constitutes a 'level playing field' in assessment, teachers could initiate discussions in their classes that explore the contested and contradictory elements of popular discourses about affirmative action, equal treatment and the 'fairness' of assessment arrangements in their own courses.

In what follows, we explore particular assessment practices that further complicate the taken-for-granted meanings of operating on a 'level playing field'. Our discussion reveals the ways in which students try to accommodate and reconcile competing discourses about what is considered to be 'fair' and 'unfair' assessment.

Granting extensions

Teachers tread a fine line when deciding which personal circumstances (if any) to take into account without being perceived by students as having acted unfairly – and the subject of granting extensions perhaps exemplifies many of the concerns of students.

Many students are concerned about the due date of assignments and what leeway, if any, there is for late assignments. This includes the granting of extensions. In line with the findings of Drew (2001), there was much variation in opinion among the students interviewed about whether teachers should adhere to deadlines; some students view moving deadlines as unfair, while others appreciate the flexibility.

Most universities have policies that explain what are considered appropriate grounds for an extension of time to be granted to complete an assessment piece. The policies usually also state how students are to apply for extensions, often directing them to submit the request in writing using a designated form and providing evidence supporting the claim. This is usually required within a certain time frame before the submission date of the assessment item.

Students generally do not have issues with the granting of extensions per se, although most can cite examples where extensions have been granted that, in their minds, were not deserved. Darren illustrates this:

When you're working and you know that someone else hasn't been pulling their weight and they get themselves an extension it's unfair. It's unfair that the student knows how to pull the strings and the lecturer doesn't know it [that the student is pulling strings].

Many students do not support last-minute, blanket extensions being given to a class, viewing it as an unwarranted benefit for those who are disorganized. Again, Darren elaborates:

> That's unfair [if a class extension is given on the day assignments are due]. Even if you worked to the last minute and you do it that night and you wake up in the morning, you haven't slept. If you've been working for weeks to get it done . . . [then the extension is] obviously unfair.

However, not all students are disparaging of blanket extensions. Others are less concerned, as Nathan suggests:

> It doesn't worry me really. It doesn't worry me, sort of thing. I actually like the extra time to polish my piece anyway. Like I will get there [to hand the assignment up] and I might be a little disappointed in what I've done, just thinking, like I could have done better [so getting an extension is a bonus].

Students also have different views about the justification they should provide when asking for an extension. Some support the idea of granting extensions without any justification and others believe there needs to be a good reason. An example of the latter is Ian, who refers to this as a 'good excuse'. Opinions range from support for granting extensions to individuals simply because a student asks for one, to expressions that students need to have a 'good excuse' for not meeting deadlines:

> I mean why should that person [get an extension for having run out of time]? There's so many other students that are in the same boat, everyone's in the same boat, you've got a time management issue there, it's critical. I've only ever asked for one extension; it was granted. But yes, if they haven't got a good enough excuse, then I don't see why. Because I'm a bit older, I know that you've got to prioritize things, otherwise you won't do any good at all.

Louise thought that she was treated unfairly when she requested an extension due to illness and was only granted a one-day extension:

> And he was really unfair – I was very sick during one of his courses and applied for an extension. I had a medical certificate for nearly two weeks and he gave me a day [laugh] and that's when it started, the real unfairness started then. It wasn't on as far as I was concerned. I'd been really sick with asthma and eligible for an extension and he wouldn't give it to me and that's when it started. I mean if it had been someone else he would have but because it was me he wouldn't.

Given that we now know how varied students' opinions are on the fairness of granting extensions, teachers might find it useful to discuss the matter with their classes. This would increase students' understanding of the diversity of opinion among their peers. By increasing this understanding they would then begin to see that the apparent 'clear cut' nature of policies and procedures is not so 'clear cut' for teachers who have to deal with requests that sit outside of a policy.

Beyond the issue of granting extensions, it appears that a further three main factors are important to students when they talk about a 'level playing field'. It is important that:

- their work is marked on its merits;
- there is consistency in marking;
- there is consistency of information.

Marking work on its merits

Most students expect teachers to apply the same marking criteria objectively to the work of all students. This is illustrated by Nadine: 'The idea is that it is supposed to be a level playing field, that we all come here regardless what age and experience and the marking criteria is applicable to everybody regardless of that age and experience.' This means that in a 'level playing field' an assessment item should be marked for what it is, and consideration of who submitted it should not influence the grade awarded. A number of students express concern that 'who they are' gets taken into account when work is marked, and that their work is marked more harshly if the teacher does not like them.

One student we interviewed claimed to know another student who tested his theory that the teacher did not like him and marked his work negatively. He submitted 'other people's work and hand[ing] that up to the lecturer . . . Work that was previously a D grade would be getting a C or P1. You can assume that it is based on the student and not the work'. Interestingly, the students did not consider a range of other possible explanations for the marking discrepancy. They did not think that the teacher might have been inconsistent or unskilled in marking, or that the criteria might have been unclear, therefore making it difficult to mark consistently. They assumed that it was because the teacher did not like them or did not expect them to produce higher quality work.

It is necessary to reiterate here that this is the perception of students – if they believe they have been assessed according to who they are, and not on the merits of their work, it is the reality for them. The challenge for teachers is to make sure that there is no reason for students to have the perception that they are being marked for who they are.

Students with a range of abilities have issues about whether their work is being marked objectively. It is not just the 'poor performers' who have concerns about their work being marked objectively. Samantha had outstanding results throughout the three years of her undergraduate degree, rarely receiving less than a high distinction for an assignment. Samantha sought feedback on assignments that were awarded the highest grade possible to see how she could improve. Yet, despite being successful, Samantha still feels that her work was not always marked on its merits:

> I'm saying in terms of assessment, I think there were a few times that people had actually graded me because they – according to what they thought I should have done on that particular piece, as opposed to what I did, as saying, 'oh well, I would have thought you would have done this or this, why didn't you?' and yet Fred Bloggs didn't do half of what I did and yet got the same grade. And I find that unfair, yeah. I think a lot more was expected of me and yet I met the essential criteria, so therefore, again coming back to that, I should have been graded just on that and not who I was or what my past history was . . . If you know the person there could be some subjective emotional type of attachment that's coming in when you're actually marking the assessment. Or you know their history. So for example you know that 'Johnny's last piece of work was a piece of trash. Isn't this fantastic, what an improvement, I'll give him a high distinction'. Whereas if you compared Johnny's work to mine, there's a big difference.

Whether 'Johnny' did get a high distinction or not for work that was of a lesser quality than Samantha's work is not the issue here: what is important is that Samantha perceives it this way. High-achieving students often feel that the expectations teachers have of them are higher than they have of other students. Whether teachers do expect more of high-achieving students is a moot point; if the students have this perception and feel that they have to work harder for the same grade as another student, it follows that they will believe that they are being treated unfairly.

While most students seemed to credit their teachers with the ability to mark objectively – although perhaps not, as previously mentioned, with the *desire* to mark objectively – some students acknowledge how hard it is to maintain objectivity. It is a concern when a student feels that the outcome of the marking process could be connected to the mood of the marker, as Veronica suggests:

> I do think anything that is judged, you're here to do the best work that you can and depending on the mood of the person that is marking it, it can just be not marked in the manner that you would like it marked. I think the human element of that is very big . . . 'You in a better mood now? Am

I going to pass now?' Your destiny is in the hands of someone else depending on how they feel at the time, that's what I believe sometimes.

A solution that students often propose to combat the issue of markers not being objective is that assignments be anonymous, for example by submitting assignments labelled with student identification numbers only. Students believe that if work is genuinely being marked according to a set of criteria names are not relevant. This is illustrated by the following students:

> Perhaps all marking should be done anonymously to eliminate any questions of bias or favouritism.
>
> (Nadine)

> That's a fairer way to go [ID on assignments] because then there's no biases that will creep in; if you see a name, 'Oh, I expect that will be a distinction plus – let's flip through, yeah, it's got all the references, yeah, no worries'.
>
> (Travis)

> People think if they [lecturers] see their name on the assignment . . . they have a preconceived idea of what they think that person is able to do . . . whether they felt the work was marked for itself and not who they are – It's common for students to say they wished they could hand up ID numbers and not names.
>
> (Duncan)

> Yeah, like, just put your student ID number. I can't say definitely I got that mark because of who I was, I mean, I have a pretty fair idea there was a personality clash between someone I actually knew and was quite close to, and the lecturer. Like I wasn't involved in – and there was no way I could say, well, I got a lower mark because of that . . . I knew that I did.
>
> (Louise)

Given this insight into the students' thinking, it is worthwhile teachers considering accepting anonymous assignments if they mark the work of students they teach. Some universities have policies of teachers marking the work of other tutorial groups, or mixing up the assignments in other ways.

Another exercise worth trying for those who mark the work of students they teach is to mark a set of assignments without taking note of the students' names. If marking anonymously is problematic then the teacher needs to consider whether their knowledge of the student is influencing their marking.

Consistency in marking

Students expect assessment items to be marked objectively and without bias. They also want consistency in marking standards. If students perceive that one tutorial group is getting higher marks than another, and that there is not a moderating process in place, then they regard it as unfair. What many students do not realize is that with anything other than simple assessment tasks it is extremely difficult to have consistent marking standards. Leach *et al.* (2001) present compelling arguments that question the assumption that assessment can even aim to minimize subjectivity. They cite Rowntree (1987) on reliability, or consistency, in marking. Rowntree describes a situation where 15 markers assessed 15 scripts on a scale of fail, pass or credit. There was wide variation in the grades awarded, with more than half the scripts being given all three possible grades, and in no case did all markers agree. There are many other studies that document the unreliability of marking systems, and indeed many studies also show that greater experience of a marker does not increase reliability (Price 2005).

Teachers would alleviate a lot of dissatisfaction among students by being 'upfront and honest' about the impossibility of achieving complete consistency when assessing student work. Involving students in self- and peer-marking exercises is one way to promote a greater understanding of the complexity of the marking process (Rust *et al.* 2003). If assessment criteria are clear, if moderating processes are in place across tutorial groups and, where possible, the work is marked anonymously, students will have less to feel dissatisfied about.

Assessment can be thought of as having a process stage and a product stage. Issues related to marking fit within the product stage as the work has been completed and awarded a mark. The process stage of assessment – everything enacted up to the point of formal marking – is more complex, and it is here that consistency is viewed by students to be an important component of being able to operate on a 'level playing field'.

Consistency in providing information

So long as the expectations of teachers are clear, most students accept some differences in expectations across dissimilar courses. However, they are less accepting of different expectations among teachers within a course. While there is some tolerance for difference of expectations, students want consistency in the information they receive.

Students experience frustration when they receive different information compared with what other students receive, and when tutors are not consistent with information or explanations, such as what they mean by a word count, the number of references they expect to be cited, and in what circumstances (if any) they will grant extensions. If there is consistency, students see themselves as more likely to be operating on a 'level playing field'.

Ursula describes her frustration when informational justice principles are not applied in her courses:

> I don't think that's fair . . . not enough was explained in the beginning, everyone was having trouble with it and people were going up to the lecturers at different times asking them questions and I think in this case if you were young, female, attractive, you got a hell of a lot more information as what you did if you were a guy, or sort of not in – I mean that sounds really pathetic and I know it does, but if you were in the 'in group' or something, with a particular lecturer, you got a hell of a lot more information.

She suggests that this problem could be easily addressed if teachers used class time to answer common questions and queries: 'Then the lecturer should be saying, "I've had quite a few questions in classes, everyone, we're going to go over a few things so then everyone knows".'

Or, as Samantha suggests, if a teacher receives lots of questions from students, this should indicate to them that their criteria are not clear or expansive or detailed enough, and hence should be amended. Alternatively, the teacher:

> . . . should take on board what Jane asks and say to the whole class, 'Jane has just asked a very interesting question, just thought I would clarify, blah', so that she or he gives that information to all of the students, so they all have the potential to be as successful as [Jane].
>
> (Samantha)

Other ways of providing the same information to all students include scheduling discussion time in class, using online discussion forums and emailing the answers to individual queries to all students.

Consistency and clarity of expectations are very important to students, and unfortunately, it appears that some teachers, perhaps despite their best intentions, seem incapable of making their expectations clear. Veronica spoke of one such teacher:

> It doesn't let you have any belief in someone, you know, if he told five of us different things – what is he going to be like when he actually marks it? How can they answer one question so differently each time? We all talk about it, we're like 'I was told this', 'I was told that' . . . I think that is a fairness issue too. It can be unfair because it can lead you to write something in a certain way that isn't what they really wanted so it is unfair that they haven't given you the same answer . . .

Inconsistency related to what is meant by a word count – that is, what words are counted and how they are counted – and markers responses to 'under limit' and 'over limit' texts are other areas of contention for students. This was discussed in detail in the previous chapter.

Lack of consistency in what students are told about reference lists, or bibliographies, is also an issue. A particularly notable example comes from Ginny, who relates her experience in one course:

> One tutor said you had to have a minimum of six references . . . Another tutor said, no, just the [photocopied] readings that we've given you . . . and another one said, no, just use the lectures and the textbook. So there was just no consistency . . . it didn't seem to be terribly fair.

Many students spoke of their frustration about not knowing how many references were required for an assignment, particularly in their early years at university. If the number and quality of references is an important criteria in an assignment, students believe teachers have an obligation to provide guidance to them. Clarity on this matter will reduce student frustration.

Occasionally an issue of inconsistency was mentioned by only one student in interviews. This does not make it irrelevant or dismissible. Katarina, for example, feels it was 'completely unfair that there are inconsistencies within the university system such as some lecturers/tutors providing students with percentage grades and others with just the grade'. Katarina had once received a final grade that was incorrect, informed her tutor and had the grade altered. She knew it was incorrect because she was able to add up the percentages of the individual assignments. On another occasion, Katarina felt she should have received a higher grade but was unable to prove it because the tutor had not provided percentages for individual assignments – and even when questioned would not. This left Katarina feeling she had been treated unfairly.

Now, to summarize 'level playing field', the first of the six key considerations related to personal expectations and past experiences that students take into account when making fairness judgments about assessment. There is an expectation from students that for assessment to be fair a 'level playing field' needs to exist. Students do not necessarily have the same understandings as each other about what constitutes a 'level playing field'. Most feel that a 'level playing field' exists if they are treated the same as each other by teachers but that the teachers should take into account individual circumstances in special situations. Students vary in their understanding of what constitutes 'individual circumstances' that should be taken into account.

Within the 'level playing field' conceived by the students, apart from personal circumstances being taken into account, four other areas are particularly notable. First, they want consistency and clear guidance in the granting of extensions. Second, they believe that the work should be marked on its merits and that students' past achievements, backgrounds or experiences with teachers should not influence the marking. Third, students want consistency in marking standards within courses, particularly across tutorial groups. Fourth, they want consistency in the information about assessment that they receive or with which they are provided.

The nature and extent of feedback about assessment

Students' perceptions of the fairness of assessment are strongly connected to the issue of feedback. Nadine suggests 'that feedback is probably one of the most important things that determines if assessment is fair'.

Few studies have examined the meaning and impact of feedback from students' perspective (Higgins *et al.* 2002; Carless *et al.* 2006; Weaver 2006) or the role feedback plays in students' judgments of fairness (Nesbit and Burton 2006). Gipps states that feedback 'in the process of teaching, is considered to be important for two reasons: it contributes directly to progress in learning through the process of formative assessment, and indirectly through its effect on pupils' academic self-esteem' (1994: 129–30).

Outside of the student perspective much has been written on the role of feedback in students' learning. For example, Brown and Knight (1994) discuss giving appropriate feedback to match various learning approaches. Other writers, including Falchikov (1995) discuss peer feedback marking – when students provide formal feedback to their peers. This is a useful addition to the range of options available to teachers to provide diverse feedback to students.

Interestingly, when students receive very little or no feedback on an assessment task they invariably think it is unfair, regardless of the level of the grade awarded. This is because most students desire quality feedback to guide their learning (Sambell *et al.* 1997; Duffield and Spencer 2002) or at least their chance of improved grades – as demonstrated by Victor:

> You'd have to have good feedback [for assessment to be fair]. That's important, very important in the early stages of assessment because you want to know what you're doing wrong and you don't want to do it [again] next time.

Students want to know where they have made errors and to receive suggestions for improvement. This is the principle of informational justice in operation. If teachers do not provide clear and detailed information that describes how a decision was made (the grade awarded), students will regard it as unfair.

It is not the receipt of a low grade that students automatically regard as unfair, but the connection between expectation (based largely on perceived effort) and outcome. Feedback is critical here, for if the expected grade and actual grade are not congruent, one of the first things students will examine is the written feedback. As these students explain:

A number of lecturers and tutors will give quite a good amount of feedback and quality feedback, comments, and some will just give you a grade and you really have no idea how you could have improved. Those people also tend to be the ones who, if you go and ask them, they won't give you anything verbally either . . . also the fact that in the same course, one tutor might give feedback and another tutor may not . . . you really don't know how you can improve, or what area you really grasped well and [that] you need to improve in another area.

(Ginny)

There's nothing worse than getting a few ticks, 'Yes, good', or 'Could have been better', blah, blah. If it actually says what areas it could have been better [we can improve].

(Ian)

Surprisingly the same is the case for high-achieving students. They also expect feedback. A comment such as 'outstanding work, HD' is not thought adequate by high-achieving students. These students usually report exerting effort with assignments, and as a consequence of this they expect an effort to be made by the marker.

This expectation of reciprocal effort constitutes a 'psychological contract'. The exchange relationship and implicit understandings between individuals and their organizations are described as a psychological contract by Argyris (1960), Levinson *et al.* (1962) and Schein (1965). In universities, students expect that teachers will provide feedback that justifies or explains a grade. This is one side of the exchange relationship. On the other side is the expectation teachers have: that students will endeavour to learn the concepts of the discipline, engage with the course content and put time and effort into addressing the topic of the assessment item.

When adequate feedback is not provided, the psychological contract has been broken – the students keep to their side by submitting an assignment that takes them a lot of time and effort, and in return they get a substandard response – one that indicates the teacher did not invest time and effort.

Sally describes a student going to a teacher to question his mark: ' "Why have I got this disgusting mark?" and if they can't answer it then . . . that's unfair. He needs to get an answer and he has a right to know where he went wrong and why'. Travis also explains his need for feedback so that he can understand a mark 'I found that not having that comment or reasoning behind why you got that grade, makes it unfair'.

Amy once received a fail for an assignment and, when examining the feedback sheet, was alarmed to find all of the ticks placed in the 'poor' column. This did not match what she expected. Amy then compared her assignment with other people doing the course and could see that the tutor had not marked consistently. She approached the tutor, who admitted to being in a rush and randomly ticking the feedback sheet. The outcome of Amy's questioning meant a re-mark of the assignment and, as a result, half of the ticks went from poor to excellent. As Amy wrote in her email interview: 'As an external student, I didn't think this was acceptable, as I really rely on decent feedback in order to complete courses and therefore gain a degree – not just a rushed effort from the tutors!' Unlike Amy, many students do not have the confidence to approach a teacher about feedback they have received and generally accept it at face value, even if they do not understand it. The various responses students have to a judgment that assessment is unfair will be discussed in greater detail in the next chapter.

Students mainly refer to feedback as comments given upon the return of an assessment item. However, occasionally students speak of feedback as comments from a teacher looking at the draft of an assignment. As Ursula notes:

> If you're one of these students that gets onto things straight away and you've got your draft copy, then you should be rewarded. Obviously you're going to get feedback and if you incorporate the feedback into your report and change it, then, yeah, you should get a good mark.

While some students think it is fairer for teachers not to provide feedback on any drafts of assignments, most want teachers to be available for consultation regarding the assigned tasks. This may be face-to-face, or via email, telephone or online discussion groups. Students regard it as unfair if teachers do not make themselves available, as illustrated by the following:

> If you can't talk to the lecturer about your mark it isn't fair.
>
> (Pip)

> The unfairness there would happen if a lecturer wasn't available to discuss the mark after getting the work back.
>
> (Steve)

> Availability of lecturers definitely. It'd be unfair if they weren't.
>
> (Laura)

Teachers sometimes give contradictory messages about their availability for consultation with students. As Nathan explains:

> High on the list is access to lecturers, and their approachability. Like, even though they say 'you can come and see us', you're really being told that they couldn't be bothered. They say 'come in' and you ask them a question and they will give you about a twenty word answer to it and say 'Is that all?'

This influences whether students judge their teachers as caring. This is another consideration students take into account when making a fairness judgment, which is addressed later in the chapter.

The balance and variety of assessment tasks

Students expect balance and variety in their assessment tasks. Assessment is viewed as fair when assessment is balanced and varied. This is procedural justice in operation, as Louise illustrates:

> Fair assessment accounts for different people's learning styles and how they like to work. Some people like to write essays and other people like to do oral presentations. In some courses there is that choice of whether you would like to write essays or you would like to do a presentation . . . some people are better at different things. When there is a wide variety everyone is rewarded. A report, a presentation and an exam, well then, overall everyone has a better chance.

If assessment is not balanced some students, like Ginny, are unable to demonstrate their competencies:

> I might be really good at presentations, but useless at writing essays and if it's all essays, well I'm in trouble. All right, I need to build that skill but it doesn't give me anything to build confidence on. I've got one item where I know that I'm confident. I can use that to build on the others.

Ginny assumes that her teachers have an obligation to build her confidence so that she can demonstrate her capabilities. For assessment to be fair students expect balance and variety in the forms of assessment tasks. For most students this means a mixture of written assignments, presentations, exams and group work. The mix would be different for different disciplines, but the principle remains.

Group work and exams are the most problematic forms of assessment and evoke high levels of anxiety and frustration among students.

Group work

Increasingly, universities are encouraging the use of group work due to the claimed benefits of collaborative learning (D'Souza and Wood 2003). These benefits include the development of higher-level thinking skills, greater engagement in learning tasks, and fostering problem solving and social interaction skills.

However, collaborative approaches to teaching and learning are inconsistent with the highly individualized and competitive ways that students are held accountable in most other aspects of their university lives. In the discussion that follows we reveal the tensions evident in students' talk about group work.

While most students we spoke with did not like group work, there were some who did. Nathan, a student with dyslexia, describes himself as struggling at university and not particularly motivated. He finds group work beneficial:

> Yes, quite like it, because if I do it by myself, I've only got myself to be able to do the assignment, but if I've got other people, I'm obligated to get it done for them as well. I don't want to let other people down and I know my friends don't want to let me down, so you drag each other through something that you would have done on the last night before it was due. You're doing [it] three or four weeks before it's due. You're getting together and you're talking through it. As soon as you're starting to talk through things, you've got four or five people that have got input into the conversation, and you learn a lot more. It's like learning for exams with a group of people. Discussing it you learn so much more than if you're sitting there and rote learning it by yourself.

While students like Nathan understand that it is important to develop the necessary skills related to working in a group, they often do not like it. We found that students who have high standards, work hard and aspire to achieve exemplary marks dislike group work because they do not like working with the students who are not so motivated to achieve high marks. This is consistent with the findings of a study by Volet and Mansfield that:

> Students with negative appraisals and an exclusive focus on performance tended to be more self-centred and saw group assignments in terms of themselves within the group. Consistent with that approach, their regulatory strategies (often maladaptive to the group activity) displayed elements of control, direction and power.
>
> (2006: 354)

Some students acknowledge that there is also pressure on students who do not aspire to achieve high grades, and that not all students want to be in groups with high-achieving students.

While students accept that there are benefits from working in groups, many think the reason for group work is not based on sound pedagogy but that it is implemented to reduce teachers' marking loads. Given this insight into students' thinking, it would be beneficial for teachers to consider four key issues in the assessment of group work noted by Webb (1995): the purpose of assessment; clarification of the goal of group work in assessment; explication of the evaluation procedures and criteria; and finally whether all three previous issues are consistent with each other. If teachers consider these four issues and communicate them clearly to students it is likely some of their frustration will decrease.

The assessment of group work is problematic for many students. They often believe that the mark they receive for group work does not reflect the work they put in, and that some students are advantaged while others are disadvantaged by the group they are working with. All of this makes students question the fairness of assessing group work. As Ginny states: 'I don't think it's usually an accurate reflection, or an accurate assessment of the work put in by different people, or their understanding or skills.'

This dissatisfaction with the assessment of group work is reported in many studies (for example: Lejk et al. 1996; Barfield 2003; and Mills 2003). The concern among students is that assessment is often based solely on the end product. The inequity of input but equal distribution of marks is seen as unfair; the students who perceive that they put in more time and effort get very frustrated with those who do not contribute equally yet automatically receive the same mark. Karau and Williams (1993) refer to these people as 'social loafers'. Social loafing occurs when students fail to contribute as much effort to collective work as they do when they work individually. As Ginny says, 'if there were the two components to it: what is the end result/the content, and [what is] the process . . . if there was a mechanism to check the working together process, I think that that would be fair.'

This is consistent with Chapman and Van Auken's (2001) findings that students were more likely to have positive attitudes about group work if they had teachers who discussed group management issues and used methods to evaluate individual performance within the group. It also resonates with Burdett's (2003) study, where students' suggestions about improving group work were mainly related to improving time management and communication, and improving assessment practices.

Interestingly, a recent study conducted by White et al. (2005) showed that many factors other than a dislike of non-performing members influence undergraduate students' feelings and attitudes toward group work and group assessment, such as social anxiety and conflict avoidance. Another issue we found that students have with group work is finding common times when all members are available. This is particularly difficult for students who have paid work or carer's responsibilities (McInnis and Hartley 2002).

In Ian's experience, group work was positive because he was assessed as an 'individual, as well as the group, so it's virtually like two marks are given out, one as the group and one as the individual'. Even if students are not given 'two marks', they think group work is fairer if they have a chance to confidentially give feedback about each members' contribution to the group effort. When students have the opportunity to comment on the contributions of members of their group they are satisfied that procedural justice principles are being followed, even if it does not influence the outcome.

Does it make a difference to students' satisfaction levels if they choose their own group? Students have varying opinions about whether it is fairer to choose their own group or be allocated to one. Generally they want to be in relatively small groups of a maximum of three or four students with others who are compatible, which to them means having a similar work ethic, similar goals and similar academic standards. They feel this is more likely to happen if they get to choose their own groups. However, this is not always the case. As Ginny indicates, she initially thought the answer to group problems was to let students choose their own group, but since having a much worse experience with a self-chosen group she is not sure. Other students are more philosophical about working in a self-chosen group, and suggest they would accept a higher level of responsibility for their own actions than if they were allocated to a group. Laura illustrates this:

> You've got no one else to blame really. Like, you chose your group and you're sort of stuck with it, you either pull together [or you suffer for it]. Like, no one is going to support you in that situation; it's your own fault pretty much. But then, I don't know, I've chosen some groups that haven't worked out and been the one doing all the work and it has not been enjoyable. But then it is my fault. I should have spoken up to that person and said 'Look, hey, you're not doing it. Get your act together.'

Blowers (2006) reports that there are problems with all of the main strategies that are used to select groups for educational projects, including students choosing their own groups. He suggests using a process that enables students to identify the skills and knowledge needed to complete a particular project. For example, a creative project might require expertise with media or language, and require some previous work experience. Through an open process facilitated by the staff member, groups are formed containing students who possess each of the requisite skills. Students do not get to select their own groups but are also not randomly placed according to irrelevant criteria – such as who they sat next to the day the groups were formed, or the alphabetical order of their name.

When group functioning is poor some students suggest that an eviction system be used to remove students who are not positively contributing to the group effort. 'Eviction' is a term perhaps more commonly used in popular culture since the advent of reality television – and it has serious connotations, such as not having the opportunity to be involved in group work and getting zero for the group task. Such is the frustration of some students about the impact of 'social loafers' on their group that they do not care what happens to the 'evicted' person.

A few students express concern about the fairness of group work in terms of the quality of the graduate completing a degree. They believe that when programmes use group work extensively, non-deserving students might graduate under false pretences. They also believe that there could be ramifications later if those students are employed as qualified graduates of the programme but may not be able to do the work required – ultimately having a negative impact on the reputation of the programme and therefore the future employment possibilities of other graduates.

Deb spoke of an even greater problem than the reputation of the programme – the reputation of the university. She described working in a group with an international student who had extremely poor written and oral English-language skills. While Deb's issue was not so much with the group mark being shared, it is an insight she only gained by working in a group with the international student:

> The issues are that she [the international student] was admitted to study at the uni with non-existent language skills in the first place, her assignments were passed in the second place, and the tutor seemed to just accept this as she had to pass the overseas students. My real issue is with devaluing our studies/qualifications, but no one seems to want to think about that. When our uni is considered a poor academic choice and the foreign students start choosing other institutions with higher standards and reputations, then the issue will be addressed.

The subject of standards within the university goes beyond the realm of this book, but it is interesting to note that many students are well aware of the disadvantages of lowering standards.

One suggestion students had to counter the problem of lowering standards with group assessments, apart from separating group and individual grades, was for course coordinators to allocate only a minor component of assessment to group work. Proposing the same argument, Nadine's case is premised on giving students the chance to make up for a potentially low mark if they end up in a group that produces work of a lower standard than an individual student would expect to achieve:

> I don't think it [group assessment] should be more than 25 per cent max because at least then people have got the chance to make up the marks to still achieve if the group effort is less than adequate or barely adequate.

To recap, group work is generally accepted by students as being worthwhile if group processes and management issues are taught and dealt with. However, the assessment of group work remains contentious. Students feel that a shared group mark does not necessarily represent the various inputs of group members or recognize the differing capabilities of those members. Incorporating some form of peer assessment or review appears to be viewed favourably, as does keeping the proportion of group marks in any one course or programme low.

Exams

It is well known that exams are generally unpopular among students (Brown and Knight 1994; Race 1995; Biggs 2003). Students we interviewed often either referred to exams as being unfair, on the grounds that they are a poor indicator of a student's capability, or they questioned just what exams really assessed. This is in accordance with Kniveton's (1996) findings that students generally regard continuous assessment as a fairer process than end-of-course examinations. Students believe continuous assessment enables them to demonstrate their ability, and provides them with more opportunities to manage their own work schedules.

Some students would like to see the removal of exams from course curricula. John, for example, claims to suffer from exam pressure and views exams as only testing memory, something at which he is not good. Another student who feels this way is Laura, who views exams as causing a decline in her overall grade.

The only student to affirm that exams were a fair method of assessment was Samantha, and this was based on the fact that students could not plagiarize or cheat, so it was the only way to know it was the work of the student undertaking the assessment:

> ... you're not able to communicate with anyone else during an exam, you're not able to get assistance, get help, to seek guidance in anyway, means that you've had to do all the background work beforehand. You have to know the answers before you walk in the door.

While Samantha claimed that exams were fair it did not mean she liked them. Ryan was the only student who spoke positively about exams, preferring them to written assignments:

> I don't mind exams. I like exams. I'd rather that than do assignments and everything ... with exams you learn it throughout the whole thing [semester] and that way you have to keep it in your head ... with literature, like you are writing it down, you just have to be good at putting words together, you don't have to really know what you are talking about ... you just find information from a computer or something.

Ryan likes exams because he is better at them than written assignments and, while some of us might disagree with Ryan's idea of what is necessary for a written assignment, he believes that he can better demonstrate his capability in exams.

For some students, exams are like a lottery: they believe that it is a matter of 'luck' whether they revise what is tested in an exam (Tang 1994; Sambell, McDowell and Brown 1997). Veronica questions the fairness of exams when students are not given some prior information about what is going to be assessed: 'You can't have to know everything you have ever learnt in a semester and go through it in two hours. That's ridiculous.'

Students express a number of other concerns with exams. The two dominating issues are, first, the lack of feedback from exams, which does not allow them to learn from the process; and second, the level of stress they experience. They believe it becomes more of a test of their ability to cope with stress than their understanding of the content of the course. Ian questions where the learning actually happens:

> Like, we're always having exams where it's say 50 per cent of the marks of the assessment, whereas the stuff you do during the semester is worth 50 per cent as well and I think a lot more is got out of the stuff during the semester than exams.

Despite all of their criticisms, most students are reconciled to the fact that exams will remain a component of assessment for many courses.

Many students consider the weighting of the exam compared with other assessment items in the course, and whether this weighting is proportionate to the perceived learning gained from other assessment types. Many students believe that within one course around 30 per cent is appropriate; greater than 40 per cent for any one type of assessment is considered unfair because it places too much emphasis on that type of assessment. Some students who have experience of open-book exams reported preferring these because it encourages them to keep comprehensive, organized lecture notes throughout the course, removing the emphasis on memorizing – hence testing them more on their understanding and application of concepts.

Given students' dislike of exams it might be worthwhile for teachers to review the role of examinations in the assessment profile of their courses. Of particular importance is the type of exam, the weighting exams hold within the course, and the information students are given about the content of the exam.

The relevance of assessment tasks

Students' perceptions of the relevance of an assessment item influence their judgment of its fairness. What is considered relevant is strongly linked to what they believe are workplace demands. McDowell and Sambell (1999: 73) found that students they interviewed regarded a fair assessment task as 'one which asks them to carry out a reasonable task, perhaps one which relates to the "real world" and measures what they see as genuine learning'. The 'real world' for many students is the world of the workplace.

While a connection to future career is most important, students do not judge relevance on this alone. They might mean relevance to life, to personal development – even to this century! Students are particularly upset by what they view as outdated assessment tasks. Students equate relevance with 'necessary', 'appropriate', 'legitimate', 'useful', 'able to be used later in life' and 'concerns me'. If students do not see the relevance of a task, they get frustrated and annoyed.

Students contend that perceived relevance is essential for them to be motivated to learn; this has also been shown by Hadzigeorgiou (2001) and Crossman (2004). Students are less likely to invest energy in real learning if they feel it has to do with 'useless information'. If they view an assessment task as artificial, unrealistic or 'missing the point', they report being 'turned off' and regard it as unfair that they should have to use their time studying things that they do not believe are relevant.

Students understand that they need a variety of competencies and that assessment should measure more than the recall of knowledge (Dochy *et al.* 1999). One such competency is the ability to work in teams, so even students who dislike group work and speak of the unfairness of it accept it. They are not entirely happy about it, as the 'but' at the end of these quotations illustrates:

> I do understand the benefits of group work and I think these days more and more everywhere you go in the workforce you see people are getting into work things and into teams and things. So people are having to understand that they can't be in their own little world any more, even if they are a specialist in a particular area; somewhere along the line they're going to have to work as a team. So I think it's valuable that we do that in university environment but . . .
>
> (Samantha)

> It is pointed out that working in teams is part of what is going to happen when you get out in the workplace. You're going to get put with people you don't necessarily want to work with, so in that sense I can see how it is good but . . .
>
> (Olive)

Similarly, students who acknowledge that some workplaces will require public speaking and presentation ability believe that the associated skills should be learned and assessed at university, despite the fact that many find them stressful. Students can see the fairness of exams if they think that the career they are preparing for will put them under similar pressure to that of the exam. The same argument of relevance is sometimes used by students to claim exams are not fair because, in the careers they foresee, they do not believe instant recall and working without resources will be a reality. The following students illustrate this point:

> Rote learning, two days later I've forgotten the whole thing. In life, in general, there is always going to be a book that you can refer to, or your

lecture notes that you took at university or someone you can ring up and say, hey, you did this as your elective or as your major, can you help me out? I see no point in putting students under stressful conditions and saying you have to answer this.

(Polly)

I think another place that exams fall down is that when you are in the workplace it is very, very rare that you don't have some form of resource, the internet for example, you know, some resources that you can use, you can ask somebody something . . . You are rarely there by yourself; you can have books; you can get someone on the phone; you can use other people to get that information. You don't have to know everything about your job in your head.

(Veronica)

Some students will accept a higher workload if they feel the assessment item is particularly relevant. As Olive says:

I'm doing this assignment for a reason. I should be getting something out of it; I should be able to take something away from it. I think there should be things that are relevant that you may use later in life, like we've just done 'X' and even though we've all whinged and complained about it, it is a lot of work and I think a bit too much has been expected of us as first time 'X-ers', it'll probably be very useful in the long run.

While students do not express the view that producing individual written assignments per se is unfair – unlike group assignments and, even more so, exams – students still talk about issues of fairness associated with the assessment method. The irrelevance of a written assignment, the lack of clear criteria for assessing it and the lack of quality feedback associated with a grade are issues that dominate students' discussion of the unfairness of individual written assignments.

Skilful teachers

Teachers are intricately, and often indirectly, implicated in the four key considerations addressed thus far. Here they are directly implicated, as teachers' skills are considered by students when making judgments about the fairness of assessment.

Students are aware that teachers have different styles and abilities, and that their approaches to teaching result in different types of learning. It is extremely frustrating to students that some teachers are perceived to be inept, yet continue to be employed, as Ursula illustrates:

The differences in the lecturers, the way they mark, the way they teach, why are they so varied? Why are some excellent lecturers and excellent at teaching and others are just so . . . others are just the opposite? Why is there such a big difference and why do we seem to notice it and others [university management decision makers] don't? It just gets passed, or it just keeps continuing on and on and on and I think that's why students say 'I'm paying for this, you know, this isn't right'.

Students sometimes become very angry with the perceived lack of skill of some teachers. Students' perception of their teachers' attitudes is a significant factor when they consider the skill of a teacher. Teachers with an attitude that is perceived by students as arrogant are most unpopular. For example, Tom, in recounting an experience with a lecturer, says 'he was unbelievably bad you know. Just what he is presenting, as if it's the only truth on earth . . . sort of an arrogant attitude . . . I just think he's an arsehole and he should not teach'.

Deb initially commented on the skill, or lack of skill, of a teacher but by the end of the conversation we realized that what annoyed her even more, or at least what drove her to lodge a complaint, was the teacher's attitude:

In my first or second semester I had a problem with the way lectures were presented in course X. The lecturer could not use the digital overhead projector linked to the computer systems, so he would put up overhead slides on a manual overhead projector. These were not readable past the first row of the 100 seat lecture theatre, and also tapered off to a narrow point at the bottom. The lecturer was the head of the course [a course with a title in it that would presume staff would know how to use recent technology], so I found it amazing that he would not avail himself of the technology. I asked him if he could use the digital projector, and he rudely dismissed my concern and told me to sit in the front row. Clearly not all students could do that. So I complained to a student advisory officer in the student association. I was more pissed off with his attitude than anything.

(Deb, email)

Many students attribute their success in a course to the skill of their teachers. Gemma is a student who failed a course, which she felt was due to her teacher not liking her because of her poor attendance in class. Gemma is repeating the course and she suggests that her success the second time is due to a range of reasons, including the fact that she is trying harder, but what is evident is that Gemma believes that the teacher is playing an important role in her success:

This time I have a different tutor who is much nicer, as the first one was bitchy. With my tutor now I feel she is really interested in what she is teaching and she is very knowledgeable about the topic. I have learnt heaps from her and from discussion in the class [with other students].

(Gemma, email)

Similarly, Darren is convinced that what he learns as a student is directly influenced by the quality of his teachers:

We had a course last year and in the lectures we learnt nothing but in the tutorials we learnt everything [the tutor was not the lecturer] and if we were to have a course with two separate classes with one taught by lecturer X and the other taught by lecturer Y everyone would go to X's classes because they would want to be in that class. They'd be getting very different lessons and they would be learning a lot. With lecturer X I might get a C and with lecturer Y I might fail.

Characteristics of skilful teachers

What do students consider to be the characteristics of a skilful teacher? From the four considerations discussed so far, a skilful teacher coordinates group work well; provides understandable and helpful feedback on assignments; provides clear assessment criteria; has relevant assessment items; and marks consistently and without bias.

We found that students also regard skilful teachers as those who:

- are able to motivate and engage students;
- are able to direct tutorial discussions;
- are good at explaining concepts;
- have a low failure rate.

Many students believe that a skilful teacher can really *motivate students*. Much has been written about the link between motivation and assessment, including using assessment for extrinsic and intrinsic motivational purposes (see Trotter 2006). According to many students, it is the teacher's responsibility to motivate them: either by the way they teach or the type of assessment they set (for example, 'relevant' assignments). Indeed, many students think it is unfair if their teachers do not motivate them. As Steinmetz notes, 'an exciting and visual delivery style and mode are simply assumed to be "standard fare" in the classroom' (2006: 3).

Students report not being motivated by a person they dislike or who has a way of teaching that they dislike. Darren, along with a number of his class members, had great difficulty with a lecturer in a core course that many failed:

I had a very negative attitude toward it from the start and then again a lot of students I've spoken to, their attitude toward their work is to do with the lecturer. If they don't like the lecturer or they don't like the way they teach it is almost like 'I'm not going to do your work, I'll leave it to the last minute'.

When motivated they will put in extra effort. Ryan speaks passionately of a lecturer who motivated him:

I did that with course Y. It was the hardest course I have ever done . . . every night I was doing four hours of homework and I loved that class . . . the lecturer would come to class with a big massive smile . . . he was telling us stories [related to the content of the course and the lecturer's life] . . . the reason I tried hard was because I loved that class and he was one of the best lecturers I have ever had.

Alise was also motivated by a tutor to work harder, wanting to prove something to the tutor and herself:

Proving something to yourself [getting good grades]. When you have a very good tutor it is maybe proving something to him or her as well . . . and looking at the possible consequences, analyzing this, what could happen if I fail for example.

Students rely on teachers to motivate them. For example, Nathan believes he 'failed "course H", because it just wasn't made interesting. What I did out at [another institution], I got a distinction'. Nathan went on to describe how a teacher at the other institution made the course interesting, and how it made the difference to him and his ability to apply himself.

As can be seen from the next excerpt, Nathan does not consider himself a particularly motivated student, and for him there is a connection between his interest level and what he views as good lecturing:

Personality and a few other things. I'm not a particularly good studier. I learn a lot more from just sitting in lectures and listening. I am not particularly motivated. Some courses I am and other courses I'm not – a complete curve of whatever I'm interested in and with the lecturers, I suppose, that's a big contributing factor, how good they are at lecturing.

If students believe that teachers are responsible for motivating them and they do not motivate them to the level that they expect – and then they receive a low mark in an assessment item – they regard it as unfair. In the students' minds, teachers who fail to motivate their students do not give them a chance to demonstrate their capability.

University teachers are responsible, within a policy framework, for setting the assessment tasks, deciding on the due date, allocating the weight of the task, selecting the marking criteria and so on. Many students would like to add 'motivating students' to the list of responsibilities for which teachers are held accountable.

So, how are teachers meant to motivate students? According to the students, they should make the course interesting, present it in interesting ways and design assessment items that interest students. If a course is boring, or not made interesting, students blame the teacher. Students regard some teachers as being interesting and able to motivate them, while students are almost polarized in their opinions about other teachers. Nadine spoke in defence of a teacher many students regarded as boring and hopeless – the two words were often used synonymously. Nadine feels the students were being harsh and that their attendance was so poor that they could not properly judge the teacher anyway: 'the minute the lecturer said we didn't have an exam [early in the semester] three quarters of the class disappeared, and then they validated it by saying "oh yeah, hopeless lecturer". Well they were never there so how do they know?'

Theories of academic motivation recognize that a range of behavioural, cognitive and social factors influence student motivation. Motivational theories in education, including two of the most well-known theories – the expectancy-value theory and achievement goal orientation theory – acknowledge the importance of the nature of learning tasks (Anderman *et al.* 2004). The expectancy-value theory addresses four components of achievement values. In terms of academic tasks, this suggests that students will be more likely to engage in a task that they perceive as important, interesting, useful, and worth their time and effort (Anderman *et al.* 2004: 3). It is the teacher who has responsibility for instructing relevant and interesting learning tasks.

Gorham and Christophel (1992) found that some teacher behaviours clearly decreased motivation. This was the case with Alise, an international student studying in Australia for one year. She talks about the behaviour of a teacher whom she found very annoying and who initially deterred her from speaking in tutorials:

> I had a tutor in a course, he was the lecturer and the tutor as well; every time he spoke about my country in his lecture he would point at me and say 'you should know that, you should know that'. I found this quite annoying, so the more he did this the more I kept my mouth shut because, I don't get angry a lot but when I do it would have extra bad consequences, it would be stupid, so I just didn't do anything. It kept on going in lectures and tutes [tutorials] . . . I was just so annoyed . . . I was angry at myself as well because I didn't respond. I'm pretty sure he thinks I'm stupid. So what I did . . . I went to his tutes a couple of weeks ago and I prepared the questions so well every time he asked something I answered and I really wanted to prove to him, now you are going to shut your mouth . . . It worked.

The negative actions of the teacher did not ultimately deter Alise, but many students would have been less able to cope with such perceived victimization.

In a study by Gorham and Millette (1997) students attribute their motivation to factors they bring with them to a course, such as: self-concept, attitudes towards the course or type of learning environment, a desire to become proficient in the specific skills that the course is expected to focus on, and their own expectations of success. Yet the students in our study attributed demotivation to teacher behaviour – most frequently mentioning a lack of teacher enthusiasm and poor skills in presenting information, followed by a lack of satisfaction with assignment outcomes (often from perceived unfair grading). In Gorham and Millette's study, a third cluster of demotivational factors is related to 'methodological or course design conditions' (1997: 246). These include classroom variety, student involvement, instructional activities and direct feedback. We would argue that much of this third cluster is viewed by students as within the control of the teacher and connected to that teacher's behaviour.

Students believe the ability of a teacher to *run tutorial discussions well* is important, especially when an assessment mark is attached to the student contribution:

> If the tutor directs people to talk I guess it can be marked but if the tutor is not making an effort to make sure everyone gets to comment then I don't see why it should be marked because it will come down to character not skill. It'd be unfair, unless you're encouraged.
>
> (Pip)

Students have very mixed views on assessing tutorial discussions. Some suggest that two conditions should operate: first, the teacher should provide strong guidance in the discussions, so that the less opinionated or less extroverted students get a chance to speak and other students are not allowed to dominate; and second, the group size should not be so large as to be intimidating.

Some students describe themselves as contributors in tutorials, and express dissatisfaction with others whom they view as 'bludging', 'sponging' and not contributing – all the while taking notes and getting ideas. They feel this is unfair because they have prepared well and shared their findings in class, and yet they feel the other students who have not done this work benefit. They claim that a skilful teacher would not allow it to happen; a skilful teacher would make all students accountable.

Students regard skilful teachers as those who are *good at explaining concepts*. While students recognize that most teachers are knowledgeable about what they are teaching, they want them to be able to 'get the message across', to present the knowledge in a way that they can understand. Teachers must be capable of communicating with students. Smith *et al.* suggest that students consider an 'ideal' professor to have 'the personal characteristics of *knowledgeable* and *enthusiastic*, the interpersonal characteristics of *empathetic* and *approachable*, and the class-related [classroom-related] characteristics of *good speaker*, *encourages interaction*, *moves about the classroom*, and *uses expressive voice*' (1994: 18, original emphasis). As Pip says: 'If they can't provide that [good communication] or do that then it would become unfair because they are disadvantaging the students by their inadequacy or their inability to do their job.'

Most academics would be familiar with students' complaints that some teachers are too abstract and theoretical. Darren makes this point:

> Everything he talks about he knows really well but he can't get it across to the students and we had an assignment to do this year and week by week we had to be taking stuff from the lectures to put into it but week by week you'd go away from the lectures and not know what to put in. He knows what he is talking about but he can't get it [across to the students].

Some students believe that they should be explicitly 'talked through' the work that is expected of them:

> I think it's unfair to throw all this work on people and then not explain it and not walk them through it, especially when they [students] come from a different educational background [not having studied mathematics at school and it being assumed knowledge for the course]. They just scare the living daylights out of you. It is so unfair.
>
> (Nathan)

Students regard skilful teachers as those who have *low failure rates*. Even though students articulate a perceived inequity in the difficulty of courses, they still believe that most students should not fail and, if this does occur, they tend to regard the failure as a reflection on the skill of the teacher. For instance, Veronica had been complaining about a particular teacher, and in attempting to describe exactly what she felt was unfair she said: 'Half of the class failed the first half of the exam. I don't think that is good; that's not fair. You don't have that many people fail without a reason.'

When students become aware of teachers who have high failure rates, they often avoid being taught by those teachers. They do this by guessing when the staff member is going to be on leave so they can do the course when it is taught by someone else; organizing international exchanges and avoiding the course altogether; and finding plausible reasons that would be approved by the programme director to do a similar course through another university.

In summary, students make direct and indirect connections between the skill of teachers and the fairness of assessment. In addition to the skills and qualities discussed earlier in this chapter – such as coordinating group work well, providing quality feedback, setting relevant and varied tasks for assessment, marking consistently and without bias – university students regard skilful teachers as those who can present content in a way that students understand, who can direct tutorial discussions and who possess the ability to motivate students. They also look for more global measures of teacher quality, such as course failure rates.

Teachers displaying a caring attitude

It is important to students that their teachers care about them. Teven and McCroskey (1996) describe the concept of 'perceived caring'. They maintain that it is important for teachers to communicate in such a manner that students perceive that they care about them. Teven and McCroskey suggest three factors are likely to lead students to such a perception: empathy, understanding and responsiveness. If a teacher understands and respects a student's view; comprehends a student's ideas, feelings and needs; reacts to the student's needs or problems; and is attentive to the student, they will be perceived to be caring.

In this case, students apply interpersonal justice considerations. As we discussed earlier, interpersonal justice relates to how people are treated (Greenberg 2005), and this includes whether they are treated with respect and dignity (Bies and Moag 1986; Colquitt 2001). We argue that if teachers do not display a caring attitude, students are more likely to consider assessment to be unfair.

Characteristics of caring teachers

Students perceive that caring teachers:

- are approachable
- display empathy
- engage with students
- assist students with greater learning needs.

We begin the discussion with *approachability*, one aspect that students consider when deciding whether teachers care about them. Inherent in approachability is that teachers have to make themselves available. Krause *et al.* found that:

> ... only half of respondents agree that staff are usually available to discuss their work and there remain a substantial number who do not perceive staff to be accessible. A little less than one-third of students feel that teaching staff take an interest in their students' progress and give helpful feedback.
>
> (2005: v)

In the organizational justice literature, this consideration of students would be connected to procedural, interpersonal and informational justice. Teachers might make themselves available to students through the use of student consultation hours or other means, but if students do not view them as genuinely approachable, they regard it as unfair. This resonates with points made by Clayson and Haley (1990), who suggest that 'accessibility' has more to do with personality than office hours.

The students interviewed articulated how important it is that they could speak with teachers without fear of being ridiculed. Many students can give examples of times either they, or another student, felt intimidated or ridiculed by teachers – which leads students to form the perception that those particular teachers are not approachable. Students are extremely reluctant to seek help from people that they think are going to treat them with disapproval and regard it as unfair if they have no option available for help or assistance with an assessment item. As several students comment:

> They're not helped through it. Like the tutors aren't there properly and the 'course b' lecturers were more interested in themselves and writing out – yeah, and people just go, 'Wow, where do I start?' And you ask them a question and they just go, 'such and such a page in the book, look it up, don't be so lazy', or whatever and you look at the book and you just go, 'Oh all right, I wouldn't have a clue where to start'. You've got no one to turn to.
>
> (Nathan)

> Students put their hand up to ask and he'd say 'I don't want to hear any stupid questions'. Somebody would ask a question and he would go 'That is stupid, stupid, stupid'. So no one would ask a question again because you were going to get called stupid in front of the class.
>
> (Darren)

> That person actually stood in front of the whole class and ripped into everybody saying, 'Look I should have failed a number of assessments, but I didn't' and then read out excerpts from everybody's paper and rubbished them, ridiculed them and after about, he'd done about four, he looked at me and said, and very snidely, 'Well congratulations, you got a distinction, there are only two in 900'. I felt that was totally unfair. I thought that if I'd done well, then it should have been acknowledged and he had no right to make that comment, because everybody in the class then was anti me, because they were all being abused and he, in a negative sort of way, gave me some praise. I thought it was totally unfair of him to read out everyone's paper, or parts of everyone's paper. It was dreadful.
>
> (Ginny)

Having the opportunity to discuss an issue with teachers might not change the grade but there is an increase in understanding, and this will most likely make the situation seem less unfair:

> If someone is approachable . . . have some sort of communication, it's got to make things probably fairer in the end. Whether it changes anything or not, at least you've got understanding. Whereas if there's no understanding, you can't approach those people or you don't feel you can, then, yeah, it [fairness] goes out the window.
>
> (Travis)

Samantha explains that if she perceives a lecturer as not approachable, this can influence her motivation to do an assignment, and her response when the marked assignment is returned:

> If, however, the assessment criteria is poorly written and I need to go to the lecturer and perhaps that lecturer's personality is not necessarily very approachable, then that could factor into how . . . motivated I am, [to] do the assignment in the first place, it may factor into my response when in fact I get that assignment back and my perception of the grade and how I did . . . A bit like customer service really, isn't it? You know, those first few seconds are the most important. If you smile at a customer and make them feel welcome, even if they've got a huge problem, the likelihood is that they're going to feel a lot better when they're walking out the door. I think it is the same in the personality of the lecturers.

Recently Emanuel and Adams (2006) used a customer service perspective to determine the dimensions of service that students associate with excellent teachers and instruction. The five dimensions are:

- tangibles (things like appearance of classroom, student seating and so on);
- reliability (teachers' ability to instruct the course dependably and accurately);
- responsiveness (teachers' willingness to respond to students' questions and concerns);
- assurance (teachers' knowledge and ability to convey trust and confidence to students);
- empathy (the caring and individual attention the teacher provides to students).

> (Emanuel and Adams 2006)

They found that reliability and responsiveness are the most important dimensions of instructor service to students, concluding that students 'place strong importance on instructors' willingness to help students, to listen to and be responsive to students' questions and comments, and to be available for appointments with students' (542). While Emanuel and Adams use the term 'available for appointments', we suggest that 'willingness to help students, to listen and be responsive' alludes to being approachable.

If students receive a lower mark in an assessment item than they expect, and they hold the belief or expectation that teachers should be approachable, the students will regard it as unfair if teachers are not approachable to the degree they expect.

While students believe that skilful teaching staff *display empathy*, this is also a quality of caring teaching staff. To be skilful a teacher needs to empathize with students so that the students' aspirations can be met. Caring teachers are people who are in touch with the new realities of student life. For example, they understand students' need to undertake paid work and that they might find it difficult to attend all lectures, or participate in group work outside of programmed time. A recent report (McInnis and Hartley 2002) indicated that 72.5 per cent of Australian university students have paid employment during the semester, working an average of 15 hours per week. This trend has also been noted in the United States and the UK (Gibbs 2006).

Caring teachers value all students, not just high-achieving students, honours and postgraduate students. Caring teachers say hello and look at students as they pass by, they know something about their students, and they take into account the individual circumstances that might affect their engagement with the course. Some of these are referred to in the literature as immediacy behaviours (Frymier and Houser 2000). Immediacy reduces perceptions of distance and facilitates communication between students and teachers. Immediacy is communicated through a variety of verbal and non-verbal behaviours.

For some students it is very important that teachers have empathy and understanding. It appears that the younger students and the students who receive lower weighted-average marks have a greater need for teachers to care about them than the mature-age students and the students achieving higher weighted averages. This may be due to the fact that many students begin university straight from high school, without much real-life experience. They move from a structured and nurturing school system where pastoral care often exists and academic requirements are clearly laid out for them. In contrast, university life can be lonely and alienating. The recent focus on the transition of high school students into university and their experiences in first year tells us they need structured and timely assistance to navigate their way through this crucial time period (Krause *et al.* 2005).

Another way teachers demonstrate their care is by appearing happy and enjoying themselves in classes. Ryan speaks very fondly of a lecturer he perceived as caring about students:

> He was a great guy . . . every class he came into he was half an hour late . . . he came in, he always had a joke . . . he made the effort to listen, to talk back, to actually have conversations with us . . . when you look at his face he has always got a smile, he is friendly to approach. Lecturer X on the other hand, or lecturer Y, they never look happy, so you don't want to talk with someone who seems like they don't want to talk to anyone.

Students perceive caring teachers as those who *engage* with students. Insights from our study suggest that many students desire recognition from teachers and receiving this motivates them to learn. This could be viewed as similar to ego-supportive skill, which Frymier and Houser (2000) found to be important to student learning. These skills enable teachers to connect with students at a personal level.

Effective teaching includes a relational aspect (Kaplan 2000; Anderson and Carta-Falsa 2002; Stronge 2002; Massingham and Herrington 2006; Robertson 2006; Robinson and Kakela 2006). Darren speaks about a friend who had studied with him in preparation for an individual essay they each wrote. The friend received a lower grade than Darren and, after discussing it with him, went to the teacher for feedback:

> He did go back to lecturer Z about the feedback and he said that when he got her to read over it again – now this is coming from him and could be pretty biased – it's his opinion, but she said she sort of saw a few things she hadn't the first time. In fact he just wanted to prove something. Maybe in the end he just wanted it noticed that he'd put the work in. It wasn't about the mark so much as she hadn't noticed he'd put the work in.

Darren's friend wanted recognition that he had made an effort, perhaps more than he wanted a change in the mark. Similarly, Darren relates how he hoped that a teacher would notice him working in the library:

> It's like when you go to the library when everyone goes home because they hate the campus. If you actually go to the library and you do some work you just hope maybe one of the lecturers will walk past and see you and go, 'Oh look, you're doing some work'.

Connection is part of a caring student–teacher interaction (Walsh and Maffei 1994; Gillespie 2005). A teacher acknowledging a student is a simple way to establish a connection. Students notice the smallest actions on the part of teachers: for instance saying hello in passing and acknowledging a student who is working in the library.

Darren mentions being closer in age as one possible reason why students connect more with some teachers. Indeed, some students in the interviews equated teachers who are in the older cohort as having 'been around a long time', lacking modern teaching techniques, having lost interest and not able to empathize with students. For example, John says: 'Some staff have been around too long and get stale, grumpy, disinterested [*sic*] . . . She's only been here about a year and it is obvious [she is more energetic and interesting].' In further discussions about this with John and other students, it became obvious that it was not the person's actual age that mattered as much as if they were perceived as caring:

> [In programme X] all you have to do is turn up and be a student; [you don't have to brown-nose] because the lecturers honestly care . . . And my course X lecturer is exactly the same . . . he's a dinosaur [lecturer who has been around a long time] as well, but he actually cares . . . It comes back to [the fact] that he cares.

Although concern with assessment might dominate students' lives at university and hence is of great importance to them, they also value a sense of engagement with the teachers. This sense of engagement is enhanced when caring teachers consciously make connections with their students at an interpersonal level.

Finally, students think that teachers demonstrate that they care about student welfare by *assisting students with greater learning needs*. Some students need, and rely on, teachers giving extra tuition to assist them to learn. This is viewed positively as an aspect of caring. Alise, an international exchange student now achieving good results, readily admits to having needed specific help when she first arrived in Australia:

> [Whether you are able to get help] really depends on the personality of the lecturers or tutors. Before coming here I talked quite a lot to other friends who are exchange or international students to maybe catch up some ideas and it is true that quite a lot of us had problems understanding what teachers expected from us for the assignments. It is true that when I arrived, I mean, referencing was something I had never done so I just had to do it, but you don't know how, so we were kind of lost. But . . . some tutors were really available and took a lot of their time to explain things like this.

Another example is Darren, who feels that a teacher who organizes reduced content for a lecture around the due date of a major assignment is 'taking them into account':

> Someone like lecturer X, maybe we all treat him differently because he is a bit younger but he is able to get across to the students. He can talk

to us. Maybe he takes more into account . . . One example, when we had a major assignment due with lecturer X, that lecture he didn't really organize anything, he turned up and there was only half the class there and he went 'yep, this is what I expected, so this is going to be a short one'. He sort of takes it into account.

The teachers who care enough to spend extra time with students who have greater learning needs – for example, helping students with disabilities to understand the expectations of teachers – make a big difference to their university lives.

In summary, students regard it as unfair when teachers do not demonstrate that they care about their welfare. Students regard teachers as caring if they perceive them as approachable, empathetic, open, flexible and willing to invest extra time with students. These teacher characteristics have consequences for student motivation and their preparedness to accept responsibility for their learning.

Students report being motivated to work when they perceive teachers to be caring. As Alise discloses:

Staff caring can be part of the motivation you have to work . . . I have to be honest, when you are a student and you go in a tutorial and you see the tutor caring about you or other students you feel kind of like, not empowered but, like, okay this person cares about me so even unconsciously you are going to make a supplementary effort to do the job . . . I have one very good tutor in this semester and on Friday mornings sometimes I say 'oh I don't want to go' but I say to myself 'okay, I have this tutor and I am going there' because I like him, and because it is very pleasant and I know that he cares. I just imagine him going to this tute and there are no students and I feel that if I was in his position I would be so disappointed.

Students make an investment of themselves – time, effort and emotional energy for some – when working on their assignments. As Darren says, 'you're sort of putting some of yourself across to the lecturers for marking. It's like you yourself are getting judged . . . Part of [yourself] is to be given a grade.' Students feel very vulnerable and self-conscious when handing up their work for assessment. Learning is an act that leaves us vulnerable because we open ourselves to changes in the ways we see the world (Boud 1995). If students perceive that teachers do not care about them, they begin to question why they should care about the course.

Students are more likely to accept responsibility for failing if they perceive that the teacher cares about them. The possibility that they will seek feedback is greater if they view the teacher as caring and, in receiving feedback they have sought, they increase their chance of understanding what their errors or misunderstandings are and, at the very least, preserve a sense of dignity and self-worth (Gillespie 2005). Students who place blame elsewhere – for example, with the perceived uncaring teacher – are not accepting responsibility and therefore not taking constructive action to deal with the failure.

Darren offers an insightful comment about how fairness judgments are sometimes made from minimal information: 'A student can't see the trees for the forest. Hurdles can create frustration; frustration can cloud judgment. Fairness sometimes has no chance.' Darren's answer to the problem is to get rid of the hurdles through communication. He believes some students are at a disadvantage; they are not on a 'level playing field', because they do not have the confidence to speak with teachers and therefore cannot get rid of the hurdles that create frustration and cloud judgment. A student lacking confidence will not approach a teacher who appears unfriendly and uncaring, so such a student will continue to believe they have been treated unfairly if an assessment outcome does not meet their expectation.

Georgia's perception of her teacher as someone who does not care influences her opinion, and not only about the harshness of the marking:

> I felt as though my teacher was a pretty hard marker and this was unfair. I think I felt this at first because of the teacher's attitude also in class, she was very rude and had the attitude that 'I am just here to teach you and I don't really care if you learn or not'.
>
> (Georgia, email)

This is quite different from John, who also speaks of a teacher who is regarded as a hard marker but is still considered approachable and skilled in communicating with students:

> Lecturer Z is like that [approachable]. It is the way that she communicates with students. She's a hard teacher, she's a very hard teacher . . . you don't get easy marks with her . . . I am happy with my grades. I got what I put in, and that is how it should be.

It appears that if a teacher is regarded as approachable and able to communicate with students, students are more accepting of what they view as hard marking. Sammi notes that a combination of friendliness and firmness can contribute to fair behaviour:

> I [was walking with] one of my course X students and we passed the lecturer as we were going to the library. We said hello to each other [lecturer and students] when we were going in there. She [student walking with Sammi] said 'She's the only lecturer in my three years here that I can talk to' . . . I think having that personality also contributes to the fairness because that lecturer sees people as people . . . to be a fair

marker you have to be friendly but firm. Friendly enough to say 'hello, how are you, good thank you' and firm enough, 'you are not doing "X" okay, you need to do this, you need to put in more effort, you did not do so much here'.

Conclusion

In this chapter we have presented a complex analysis of the way students decide the fairness of their assessment. It is a mixture of an individual reflective process and the social process of comparing their work with others.

Our analysis reveals an ongoing tension between meritocratic ideals that reward 'ability' and 'hard work', and concerns for the equitable treatment of students. These tensions are most evident in students' constructions and use of a common sporting metaphor, the 'level playing field'. Some students went to great lengths to try to justify a return to the classic interpretation of a level playing field, one that positions all students at university as players in an academic competition in which no students are advantaged. On the other hand, many students articulated a more nuanced and complex analysis of the often hidden factors that contribute to unfair assessment practices. These students referred to major differences between their peers due to their age, socioeconomic status, English-language abilities, race and, to a lesser extent, gender.

These competing discourses about the fairness of assessment present university teachers with serious challenges as they seek to satisfy the demands of high-quality merit-based assessment while at the same time ensuring that all students have an equitable chance to develop and demonstrate their capability. These complex issues have consequences for the ways students respond to perceptions of unfair assessment.

Chapter 5

Responding to unfair assessment

It was his attitude, being rude, that made me take it further. I got so indignant.

(Deb)

I'd go and see the lecturers and ask them why they thought it deserved that.

(Duncan)

It would probably be enough for some students to pack their bags and it could well happen, depending on how unfair it was. I mean, what experience they've had ... [If] it disturbed you in such a way that you thought, 'hey, this is just not worth it. I'm not getting anything out of this. This is too unfair' and out the door. And I know a lot of people have probably done that. They've probably thought, well, this is not the right programme for me.

(Travis)

Having explained how students decide the fairness of assessment, we now discuss students' responses when dealing with assessment issues that they perceive as unfair. This is the second stage of the theory of demonstrating capability.

There are two components to this stage. First, there are the various emotional reactions of students. The second component is the actual response of students – that is, what they do after perceiving that assessment is unfair. The response is influenced by a series of modifiers (understandings or conditions) that put pressure on the action students ultimately take.

Emotional reactions

The ensuing discussion of the emotional reactions students have to perceived unfair assessment shows that, for many students, a sense of unfairness creates highly emotional states. Students we interviewed reported many emotional reactions when they perceived assessment to be unfair. Some of the descriptors used were: 'annoyed', 'anger', 'frustrated', 'resentment', 'disgruntled', 'bemused', 'dejected', 'defensive', 'knocks confidence', 'reduces confidence', 'erodes confidence', 'cheated', 'duped', 'system against you', 'lacking control', 'victim', 'very uncomfortable', 'pull back', 'self-doubt', 'disheartened', 'knocked back', 'demoralizing', 'upset', 'confused', 'shock', 'bewilderment', 'totally pissed off', 'sad', 'lose interest', 'useless', 'drag your feet', 'disappointed' and 'cross'. For some students the emotional reactions are relatively short-lived but for others they have a long-lasting effect.

The following excerpts give a sense of how students feel when they perceive assessment to be unfair:

> Oh, it really makes you feel as if you've got no control whatsoever over the situation. You automatically assume a victim role that you've got no control, poor little me. Yeah, it's very uncomfortable. You just feel that nothing is fair, there is no equity and you pull back.
>
> (Nadine)

> Useless, yeah, a feeling of being useless, yeah. I mean that's how I felt. That's how quite a few of us felt in this one particular course, [how we felt] was useless.
>
> (Ursula)

> It reduces my confidence considerably and whilst I might appear to be a confident person, I'm not and that sort of works in the negative, because people think that I can handle negative feedback and, unless it's very constructive, I have a problem. Yeah, and it would affect my performance in the next one too.
>
> (Ginny)

There is an impact on the emotional health of many students. Nathan gives an example of this:

> I felt annoyed, to put it mildly. I was better off not even putting the effort in ... Disheartened [to get a P1 when I felt I deserved higher]. Yeah, the worse you do, I think it's a trough and the worse you do – yes, it [is compounded], if you don't try hard in the next assignment. You try really hard and you get knocked back again and you don't bother putting that much effort into the next assignment and when you do that, you get a mark back that's even worse, and then it knocks you down even further.

Nathan felt disheartened and became less motivated in future assignments because he did not see a connection between the effort he was putting into assignments and the outcome. In contrast to this, Sammi dealt with his emotions, and by communicating with the lecturer he was able to achieve a better outcome. This was not without a degree of turmoil:

> The feeling is not so good . . . to tell you frankly when I received one of my assessments where I thought I had been unfairly marked the whole of Thursday night I tried to sleep and I couldn't sleep because I was thinking about this assessment . . . So many things were going around in my head. I had to type the letter [draft email to the staff member that the student felt had unfairly assessed him], put it into the computer. When we went on a field trip I started talking with lecturer X because he had had a similar experience as me with his study so he could relate to me and it came out of me [the emotion] which was a good thing because when I came back on Monday I was more focused. I sent her another email, not that one I had typed because that one was so nasty. The second email was to me more objective and questioning. From there it developed into a better understanding, better grading or fair assessment. She altered the grade.
>
> (Sammi)

These comments show the importance of individual judgments of the fairness of assessment, because events are critical when people perceive them as such. Schein (1992) explains that there are varying levels of reality: external physical reality, social reality and individual reality. Individual reality refers to 'what a given person has learned from her or his own experience and that therefore has a quality of absolute truth to that person' (1992: 99). It is the 'individual reality' of a student that unfairness exists in assessment. If students are 'bewildered' by receiving grades that are lower than expected, or are 'disheartened' by thinking that greater effort in compiling a group report has not been recognized in comparison to the input of other group members, or are 'put out' for working hard to meet a deadline while other students are granted 'easy extensions', then those students' reality is that unfairness exists, and their emotions are often powerful.

Boud (1995) describes the experience of a former colleague teaching a course on assessment in a postgraduate programme for university teachers. At the beginning she asked them to write an autobiography focusing on their experiences of being assessed. The results were devastating and showed that even successful, able and committed students – university teachers – have been hurt by their experiences of assessment. Experiences of assessment caused the university teachers to lose their confidence, dented their self-esteem and led them never to have anything to do with some subjects again. Boud asks: 'If assessment has such a profound effect on the successes of the system, how much greater must be the negative effects on their less academically accomplished peers?' (1995: 36).

Falchikov and Boud (2007) acknowledge the importance of the emotional experience of being assessed. Clegg and Bryan (2006) claim the emotional impact of assessment is an underrated area of investigation. In the writing of this book we have had many discussions with people inside and outside the university system – every person has an assessment experience to relate and without exception these experiences are associated with strong emotions.

The emotional reactions of students are an integral part of the second stage of the theory of demonstrating capability – that is, responding to perceptions of unfairness. See Figure 5.1.

Our analysis of our data shows that students have varying levels of tolerance of unfairness. For some there is a catalyst that triggers a specific response. Before describing the actual responses, we will discuss the factors that influence the response. We have called these factors 'response modifiers'.

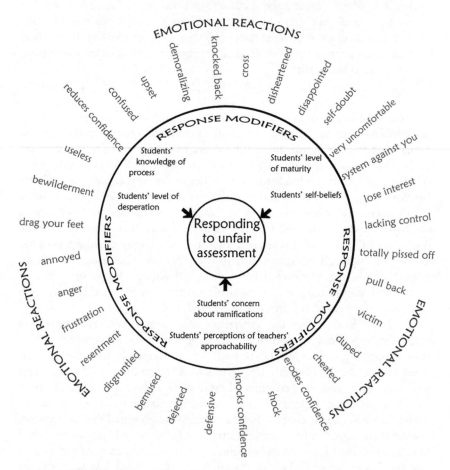

Figure 5.1 Stage two: Responding to unfair assessment. The emotional reactions and the response modifiers

Response modifiers

Response modifiers describe the conditions that influence the actions students take if they perceive assessment to be unfair. The response modifiers can change over time.

Students' responses to a perception of unfairness of assessment vary. Students make decisions about whether the unfairness is significant enough for them to take action. If, for example, Tracy perceives something is unfair she will:

> ... get all the discussion [from her peers] and if it really annoyed me I'd probably go to the lecturer and discuss it and say 'look, you know I just need to tell you this, I don't think this incident is fair because' and justify my reasons. 'Why was this?' Try and seek an answer from them and hopefully they'd be able to answer it. If not I'd go to the Head of School. I'd try not to lodge a formal complaint but I guess if something was very unfair and it got to that situation then I would.

Tracy has a plan of action depending on the perceived level of unfairness. She avoids lodging a formal complaint but will if necessary. Tracy is typical of *a few* students we spoke with.

Polly is a capable, high-achieving student, approaching graduation. She changed from one programme to another when she realized the original career path she had envisaged was not appropriate for her. Polly is clear about how university can help her to achieve her goals in life. She works hard and invests time and effort in her assessment tasks. Polly gets angry when she thinks she has been treated unfairly and she does something about it. She is more concerned about justice than getting a 'reputation' for being a troublesome or complaining student. Unlike many students, Polly will raise issues with teachers on behalf of the group of students succeeding her. The 'Pollys' in the university know the *Assessment policies and procedures manual*, and they demand explanations if they perceive unfairness. Most students we spoke with are *not* like Polly.

Alise believes students work out a strategy of action based on what they think the consequences of taking a particular action will be:

> It depends on the student ... Everyone might think about any other strategies because you ask yourself 'What are the possibilities? What can I do?', and you have all these elements, and then you take the decision according to the consequences of each of the elements. According to your personality and the environment.

Alise is strategic. Students exercise control of their learning when they assume a level of ownership of assessment. They lessen the frustration related to assessment. They ask, if they do not understand the criteria, standards, expectations or marking scheme. Their response to a perception of unfair assessment is proactive. Tracy, Polly and Alise are all examples of proactive students. They are likely to progress through university without major setbacks because they lessen any frustration they experience. Polly's actions have a positive impact on the lives of other students because she advocates on their behalf. Polly's actions might result in teachers making expectations clearer, or altering their behaviour in such a way that students' frustration with assessment is reduced.

A range of response modifiers influences the actions students undertake when they perceive assessment to be unfair. We present six response modifiers:

- students' level of desperation;
- students' concern about ramifications;
- students' level of maturity;
- students' self-confidence/sense of self-efficacy/self-concept;
- students' perception of teachers' approachability;
- students' knowledge of process.

While these are presented as separate entities in the ensuing description, there is considerable crossover between them. The response modifiers do not remain static; for example, students in their final year might be less concerned about gaining a reputation than when in first year, or they might have less need for teachers to be approachable before questioning them about an assessment item. Throughout the life of a student some response modifiers will be more significant, or have more impact on students' decisions, than others.

A response modifier might also change as a result of the action students take. For example, students might speak with a lecturer to clarify a term used in the feedback on an essay. The students might come to realize that the crux of the problem is something in their control that they can attend to in the next essay. As a result, they gain a greater sense of their ability to write essays than they would have had they not sought help.

Students' level of desperation

The response students have to a perception of unfairness is influenced by their level of desperation. Most students accept that assessment is sometimes unfair; it is part of life and only worth bothering about if it is really significant, and the significance is linked to students' levels of desperation.

What it takes for students to become desperate is highly variable. At one extreme are students who become desperate if they receive a mark for an assessment item that is lower than they expected to receive – for example, they receive a pass instead of a distinction grade. Some students become desperate if the mark they receive would mean they fail a course. The following comment from Rosie shows how her response varies with the receipt of different grades:

> If I had received a P1 but felt it deserved at least a credit or distinction I would have been hysterical and gone all over the shop to everyone else. I don't think you can fail if you honestly submit the best piece of work you can ever do . . . But if I got a P2 I'd always question. I'd be like – look, go through it with me. I'm coming to meet you at this time. I want to know why I didn't do so well and can you please help me further improve it next time?

Ian, a part-time mature age student, would only take action of any sort if he received a fail: 'But if I failed an assessment task, I'd probably be more inclined to say, to actually go back and ask what was wrong with it, more so than if I passed and was unhappy with the mark'.

There are students who get desperate 'just in time'. One example is a second semester first-year student, Maria, who had borderline passes in all courses and had not shown concern. She had not paid much attention in class throughout the study period and was one of the 'group' always passing notes to friends in the back row of the lecture theatre. Maria failed the second assessment piece of a course, an essay. She worked out that it was possible she could fail the course itself. Nothing had prompted her to seek help, but now she was desperate. She went to the teacher asking for feedback on the failed essay, saying that she was surprised to have failed and seeking a resubmission. The teacher did not allow a resubmission. She advised Maria to invest considerable time and effort into studying for the final assessment piece, an open-book test. This required that Maria go back through the course outline and complete the weekly readings, discussion questions and class exercises that she had not been doing throughout the semester. Maria admitted that she had not carefully read the course outline and assessment criteria when working on the essay. This admission enabled the teacher to offer a number of suggestions to Maria, which, if followed, would result in a more academically successful time at university for her.

It is possible that the consequence of failing the essay meant Maria prepared for the open-book test more than she otherwise would have. Maybe the shock of failing one essay changed her attitude to university work, because she went on to pass the course.

Steve is typical of students who would not generally do anything about failing one assessment item – as he says: 'It depends on the other assessment pieces as well, whether you think you could make it up in others.' Failing one item would not make Steve desperate enough to take action of any sort.

Students often say they would only 'do something' about unfair assessment if they thought it was 'important enough', and usually this meant that they were likely to fail the whole course, as these students attest:

If it depended on me passing a course I would do something, probably.

(Melanie)

It would have to be something pretty big I think, like huge . . . something affecting graduation or if I failed a course and I thought something was really wrong, I'd probably, before I could go and speak to someone about it I'd come and say is there anything else that can be done. It'd have to be something pretty big. Probably if I had support, like the majority of people as well, a group, I'd be more likely to speak out.

(Laura)

The disadvantage to students who only respond to perceptions of unfairness in situations that provoke a high level of desperation, such as failing a course, is that they limit their chances of reducing frustration. If students respond to a perception of unfairness when they are not desperate they might increase their understanding of the assessment criteria and lessen their frustration. Asking a teacher to explain why they received a particular mark for an individual assignment might result in them not failing a complete course.

There are students who only become desperate if they receive a letter of preclusion, stating that they are not allowed to continue to study at the university. In universities, under usual circumstances, such a letter is sent after a student has been notified of unsatisfactory progress for a number of academic review periods. In the case of the university where this study was conducted it is three or more academic review periods; so these students will have had a series of failed assessments. We had discussions with university counsellors and student advisory officers who were trained in providing advice and advocacy to students on a range of issues, including appeals against preclusion. It was confirmed that many students only access counselling services when the university requires them to. The counsellors made the point that seeking advice earlier would have helped many of these students.

The implications of not taking action appear more significant in students' final year, as they risk not graduating. Students often report being much more likely to do something if they were in their final year. Melanie provides an example:

Yes, in third year you'd be much more concerned because you want to pass your degree and you graduate next year so, yeah, definitely. In first year you might not even worry about it too much because you're not going to be aware of the policy and you'll probably think 'oh, I'll just repeat it next year'. I know people who'd do that.

There are many reasons why students might respond differently in higher year levels. As we have said, it is possible that their levels of desperation are more easily triggered in higher year levels, but it is also possible that other response modifiers will have changed after two or three years at university. For example, students might be able to approach teachers more easily; they might have a greater knowledge of the processes available to them; it is likely they will have a higher level of maturity; and perhaps their self-confidence will have increased. However, it is of great concern to universities that the attrition rate among students is so high that many do not reach the final year of their degree. For these reasons 'early intervention' programmes that encourage students to take action before they become desperate are increasingly important.

Belief that change might be the result

Students who are desperate take action of some sort either because they have nothing to lose or because they believe that they have something to gain. They believe that taking action is worth the time and effort. Georgia, for example, did not think the 'hassle' was worth it when she received a lower mark than she felt she deserved, as she says:

> I didn't do anything about it. I thought the whole process of actually doing something was too hard and the hassle that would have happened is not worth it. The main reason I felt this way was because I still got a pretty good mark.

Nadia did not challenge her tutor about the mark she received on an assignment even though she was absolutely sure the work was not read properly. Although she felt she should have received a higher grade she was 'very busy in life, didn't want to cause a hassle; it wasn't worth it', and she did not take it further. As Rosie says: 'The business of life can mean you don't do anything – unless you are desperate.' For students to take action it seems they need to perceive the issue to be important enough and believe that change might happen.

Earlier we used the example of Deb, who spoke to a teacher who was presenting work on a screen that could not be read by students past the first row of the lecture theatre. After speaking with him she became annoyed at his attitude even more than his inability to present legible work. Since he was also the course coordinator, she then spoke to the student advisory officer: 'It was his attitude, being rude, that made me take it further. I got so indignant.' Eventually she gave up on advocating for change, feeling that it was not worth the effort:

> Well, after 2 meetings and too many emails, which were very time consuming, basically I was told that the lecturer could do what he liked, and there were no minimum standards that he should meet. The whole

situation cost me many hours of email writing and carefully considered responses. I felt it was just not worth the effort of continuing to complain – my time is too valuable. This experience caused me to not complain about any other subsequent problems.

(Deb, email)

Deb was disgruntled because she felt that nothing could be done about the teacher's performance or attitude, and as a result of this experience is reluctant to respond to other problems.

Amy planned to follow up an issue she had with a teacher who had admitted to being in a rush marking her assignment – and had randomly ticked boxes on a feedback sheet. The teacher changed the grade immediately when he was questioned. Amy was going to write a letter of complaint once the course was finished 'but never got around to it as I thought that my complaint wouldn't have gone too far, since this person has been at the uni for some time'. Amy had done what was necessary to change her grade, but when it came to taking the issue further decided it was not worth it because she did not believe that change would result. Amy had clearly internalized an individualistic orientation to assessment that worked to discourage her from taking a more systemic form of action to address inadequacies in the assessment process.

Students' concern about ramifications

Anxiety about possible ramifications influences many students' responses. As Nathan says, 'I am always fearful that if you go and dispute an essay with somebody they will start begrudging you a little bit, in my view.' Nathan understands his – and other students' – vulnerability in an assessment regime where they have little power compared with that of their teachers.

Students interviewed often spoke with concern about gaining a 'reputation'. A pertinent example comes from Nadine, who was upset about the varied marks students received from different tutorial groups in one course. She was worried that if she did anything about it she would 'get a bad name for herself', and end up in a worse situation:

And there was a large difference in marks, we're talking about a range of six to ten marks here, for things that were identical, and so I did approach tutors and approached the lecturer, who said 'see the tutors', who said 'see the lecturer', who obviously didn't want to know and left it at that. The upshot was I'm not going to keep making a fuss; I'll get a bad name for myself. If there is anything that requires the benefit of the doubt, I won't get it, that trouble maker, so [I] pulled my head in, so did the others and we just kept quiet about it. As much as people say, yes, there's channels for recourse and everything, it's still almost like being

in the playground where you think, if I make a fuss it'll all come out
and I'll end up losing in the end.

The more official the complaint, the more students were concerned about
the possibility of being disadvantaged in their future life at university. Melanie
was apprehensive about asking for a re-mark because she would 'get off-side
with the lecturer'. These cases show the influence of implicit self-disciplining
beliefs about the relative lack of power students have in contesting assessment
outcomes.

John decided it was not worth appealing a grade because he felt there
would be ramifications, whichever way the decision went:

> You are better off not putting in an appeal because if they find out about
> it and you have to repeat the course then you have to put up with their
> crap . . . If you win the appeal and don't have to repeat the course and
> if you are lucky enough not to have a course with them again [that's
> fine], but if you get an appeal and it was granted then . . . I think that
> if in their mind they have lost a battle then they are going to [retaliate
> against] the student . . . or they are going to pass that information about
> the student on to other staff members.

John's worries were based on previous experience when he had appealed a
grade, was unsuccessful and believed that the lecturer discriminated against
him the following year when he repeated the course:

> I was repeating course Y and lecturer Z, even though in the first exam
> – because I had already done it before – the first exam I got 85 and the
> second was 88 per cent and he wrote me an email saying 'if you don't
> hand up this assignment in the next week, I don't want to fail you but
> I will' . . . bullshit, he wanted to fail me . . . It was just the way he held
> himself around me and the other students – and because of our history
> in the first time I did the course when I appealed the grade.

Some students are worried about the effect of what happens in one course
being passed on to other teachers. Ryan gives an example of a teacher in one
class starting to treat him differently. He believes it was due to an incident
in another class:

> Lecturer X and lecturer Y are pretty good friends and before that incident
> [with lecturer X] I was going pretty good in course Y with lecturer Y.
> I am pretty sure they talked with each other and I noticed a difference
> with the course Y class . . . Some of the lecturers, even when you are
> walking around they give you dirty looks, like lecturer Z and all that, it
> used to be when we started they used to be all nice, like every time you

walked past, like 'hello, hello'. Now they put their heads down and walk past you.

Ryan does not consider other possible reasons for the teachers not saying hello to him as they walk past. It is his belief that teachers discussed an incident that happened in one class among themselves and the result was that they acted differently toward him. Ryan is acutely aware of the possible ramifications of taking action.

John and Ryan's stories show that a minority of university teachers behave in ways that actively discourage students from speaking out when they feel that they have been treated unfairly. They exercise overt power to prevent students from complaining about their practice. Not all students are concerned about ramifications, however. It is Sammi's opinion that the students who are concerned about reputation are the ones who are not 'keeping their side of things':

> It will cause a problem to students if they don't keep their side, but for me I am all the time in my courses, I do my readings, I submit on time, I go out of my way to learn about this and that and whatever the lecturer is concerned about I give it back, so whatever is humanly possible I give it back. These people who are mostly frightened of such things as getting a reputation or repercussions are the ones that are not keeping their side of things.

It is likely that some students are not 'keeping their side of things'. However, many diligent students report being concerned about their reputations. Only a minority of students say they are not worried about possible ramifications. Alise, an international student like Sammi, is one of the few who are not worried:

> If I was sure that there was a real problem in this course, I would just go for it and really try to fix the problem with whoever without worrying about my personal reputation or anything . . . I think it is really character based [worrying about reputation] . . . To some people it can depend on the school and the size and the potential of analysis of others, but in this kind of problem I would say it is more likely related to personality.

Some, but not all, mature age students suggest that resolving fairness issues is more important than concerns about how they are viewed by their teachers. Polly was mentioned earlier as a student who speaks up on behalf of her peers. Veronica also reports often taking a case to a teacher on behalf of younger students, whom she sees as getting a 'raw deal':

> Some of the young kids . . . because a lot of them live at home and have just come from high school and they don't like to question. I think they

should be taught that there is a time when you can question and it is not that you have to go in and aggressively question someone. You're basically saying 'I have a difference in opinion' and start with that.

Students' level of maturity

Maturity and chronological age are often, but not always, related. Some students display great maturity in outlook and responsibility for learning at a young age. Rosie is 22 years old and reflected on her first year at university. She realizes that some of her earlier decisions were based on peer group pressure rather than educationally sound ideas:

> The older you are the less you start to care about what your friends think. I remember when I was 18 and starting uni, I was like – oh my god, I don't want to sit in the back row, can't see a thing, like the room is too dark. But I want to be cool, I want to be liked – the whole [issue of] wanting to fit in; you don't know anyone yet.

Olive (24 years old) and Nadine (36 years old) were both completing second year when we interviewed them. They felt that their response to a perception of unfairness would be a more active one as second-year students, than when in first year:

> Maybe because I was a first year and whatever last year and with that exam and I sort of just accepted that. Now I think I'd probably take it further and see what else could be done about it because that was an exam where I think over two-thirds failed.
>
> (Olive)

> Oh, if it was a really big thing like failing I would take action. I wouldn't have once, but I would now, being in second year.
>
> (Nadine)

A change has occurred from first year to second year for Olive and Nadine. Neither came to university directly from school but each needed to gain confidence at university before considering taking action. Mature age students themselves acknowledge that it is scarier for young people in their first year of university, having come straight from secondary school, to challenge or question a teacher:

> I think that comes with being older. Like, I think if I'd been struggling at school I probably would have been too scared, but I actually knew a bit more about what I was doing and where I was going and what I wanted to do. So yeah, I think that made a bit of a difference to my

approach. Whereas if I'd been like a scared first year straight from school in university, I probably wouldn't have, I would have just let it happen, let it go. Because I was a little bit older then, I didn't [let it go].

(Louise, 26 years old)

Some students mature as learners through the experience of being at university. In Darren's case this has not happened. Even when completing third year he often felt like a school student. He knows that at university students need to accept more responsibility than at school: 'We are now uni students and, after all, we have to take it upon ourselves to find out more information. It can't all be given to us at the start of the year.' Darren is acutely aware of his lack of ability to relax around university teachers and envies those who can:

But . . . people who have come from high school like myself I think treat lecturers like teachers at high school . . . but different teachers tell you off and I've had that feeling with lecturers every year, even this year. So I can't think of a lecturer and talk to them the same way as other people, especially mature age students from 'programme X'. I spoke to a couple of them and they just talk to lecturers about anything, and they're laid back and they're happy with the system, but with me I look at a lecturer . . . and it's like they're a school teacher. That's the attitude I've had towards lecturers.

Darren's maturity as a learner is perhaps being stifled by his inability to feel that he belongs at university.

Some students are goal-orientated and self-directed learners: mature in outlook and self-motivated. Part of being an autonomous learner is to accept responsibility for the learning process and realize that much of the motivation for learning comes from within. The following excerpts are from students who declare the need to accept a level of responsibility for clarifying any confusion or frustration they might have about assessment tasks:

I guess there is only so much that a lecturer could do. You write it out, offer an explanation, ask for questions and that sort of thing, then I guess the rest should probably fall back on the students, in terms of a hundred per cent clarification. A lecturer does what they think they can.

(Laura)

You should at least have gone and spoken to your lecturer if you don't know what you are doing . . . If they don't understand the question, it is up to them [students] to go and say something.

(Polly)

At university level it's probably up to the student to decide whether they
need that kind of help or not.

(Samantha)

And if there's any discrepancies – I would go and ask the lecturer about
the criteria – if there's no set criteria, or not enough, you'd go and clarify
that beforehand.

(Steve)

Indeed, some students are quite disparaging of others who they see as not
accepting responsibility for their learning, as these excerpts show:

Look I mean students, or [university students] everywhere you go, claim
unfairness, it's actually, it's just themselves, they would find everything
unfair. Just because they are lazy and they – whatever their reasons are,
you know – they always find something out there [to find unfair].

(Tom)

If they haven't realized until the week before that there were some issues
with the assignments, well, it's just bad luck as far as I'm concerned.

(Louise)

Unfair assessments . . . a lot of people have the ability to do a lot better
in assignments than they actually do, because they leave it to the last
moment, they tend to get a little bit side-tracked and they don't do it
half as well as they could. Once again, you need to be able to motivate
yourself to get it done in a work situation.

(Nathan)

While maturity includes students accepting responsibility for their own
learning, it also is connected to confidence in approaching teachers. This is
consistent with the findings of Krause *et al.* that mature age students 'tend
to have strong clarity of purpose and are more likely to seek assistance from
staff' (2005: v).

Students' self-beliefs

The earlier discussion on students' level of desperation showed that some
students only take action if the issue of unfairness is perceived to be really
significant. For other students, such as Laura, this isn't the case. Laura
describes herself as 'stand-backish': 'I'm very stand-backish. I'll go "Oh, that's
not fair", but I wouldn't do anything about it. I can't think of anything [that
would cause me to do something about it]. Yeah, I wouldn't.'

Yet other students question teachers about anything they perceive to be unfair. Veronica, for example, said without hesitation:

> I would go and see them. I'd say 'I don't think this is right'. The effect that has on me [perceiving unfair assessment] is to come forward and question it for myself and that's what I have done when I haven't been happy about something.

Another example is Alise. She got her first assignment back and did not understand the marking scheme. Without hesitating she asked the teacher for an explanation.

Students' personalities contribute to their response, or lack of response, to perceptions of unfair assessment. In attempting to understand individual differences, we examined the data and also utilized other opportunities available to us. This included when Nerilee led bushwalking and paddling expeditions with students during their outdoor recreation coursework. She was able to engage in numerous informal conversations. If the conversation turned to assessment issues, she often asked the students why they did not speak to their teachers about the issues. A very common response from them was that they lacked confidence; usually their responses were along the lines of, 'I wouldn't have the confidence to do that.'

This, in combination with many references to 'personality' in the interview data, led us to consider literature on self-confidence, sense of self-efficacy and self-concept. It helped us to understand why some students might take action, and why others do not. A brief discussion is included here about the three 'selfs'.

Self-confidence

Self-confidence is not necessarily a general characteristic that pervades all aspects of a person's life. It is not unusual that a person will feel quite confident in some areas of their life yet at the same time lack confidence in other areas. A lack of self-confidence is also not necessarily related to a lack of ability. A student might be quite capable but due to unrealistic expectations of parents, or significant others, lack self-confidence.

Sammi was successful in having his grade from a group report changed after he questioned his teacher. He heard of another group that had a similar situation of disparate grades so he:

> ... encouraged a girl to just write a small letter requesting, please, if you can consider [the grade again], and she did that and her grade was increased and she was happy. The next day she came to me and said 'oh, thank you for advising me on that'. She wouldn't have done anything if I had not heard and encouraged her ... She lacked confidence, and there were a few others [who also lacked confidence].

The encouragement from Sammi was enough to boost her confidence.

Nadia made a link between her feelings of confidence and her year level at university, knowing that in her first two years she would not have questioned a tutor because she was 'lacking a bit of confidence early on, particularly as the other students knew a lot'. However, by her third year she started to query the marking more, and now in fourth year she wants to know what she has done wrong and will 'go and talk to the tutor'. Nadia now has the confidence to approach the course coordinator, and even the programme director, if she does not get a satisfactory answer from the tutor or course coordinator.

Sense of self-efficacy

Psychological theory on human motivation has dealt with the concept of personal expectancy in many ways. Much research supports the idea that expectancy can influence behavioural instigation, direction, effort and persistence (Schunk 1991). One type of personal expectancy is self-efficacy, a concept introduced by Albert Bandura (1977). Individuals' sense of self-efficacy is how competent they feel in dealing with a given task. It is situation-specific and only able to be generalized to another situation if the two situations are very similar, unlike many other expectancy beliefs that are not so task-, or situation-, specific.

The tenets of self-efficacy have been tested in varied disciplines and settings and have been applied in diverse fields dealing with issues such as phobias, depression, social skills, assertiveness, smoking behaviour, pain control, health and athletic performance (see Pajares 1996). Since the mid-1980s educational research, primarily in the area of academic motivation, has focused increasingly on self-efficacy (Schunk 1990, 1991; Maehr and Pintrich 1991; Pintrich and Schunk 1995; and for a comprehensive list see: Pajares 1996; Pintrich and Maehr 2004).

Bandura (1993) summarizes a substantial body of research on the diverse effects of perceived personal efficacy, categorizing them into what a person with a low sense of efficacy will do compared to a person with a strong sense of efficacy. Examples are that a person with a low sense of self-efficacy will 'shy away from difficult tasks', 'have low aspirations' and 'be slow to recover their sense of efficacy following failure or setbacks'. A person with a strong sense of efficacy will 'approach difficult tasks as challenges to be mastered', 'in the face of failure heighten and sustain their efforts', and 'approach threatening situations with assurance that they can exercise control over them' (1993: 144–5).

Considering issues related to university assessment, it is undoubtedly beneficial for a student to have a strong sense of self-efficacy. Pajares (1996) reports many findings that support Bandura's (1986) contention that efficacy beliefs are often more important than skill level or other self-beliefs in subsequent performance. He suggests that efficacy beliefs rather than skill determine how much effort students apply to assessment items. Efficacy beliefs rather than skill also determine how long people will persevere if they find something difficult, and how resilient they will be in the face of failure or negative feedback. We all know of students who are capable of achieving higher marks than they do. Bandura, and many others, would suggest much of this is to do with the students having a low sense of self-efficacy as this affects persistence, effort and perseverance – all qualities that are essential in consistently achieving high-level results.

Sammi clearly exhibits qualities that demonstrate a high level of self-efficacy. He maintains a strong commitment to goals, in the face of failure he heightens and sustains his efforts, and he approaches threatening situations with the belief that he can have some control over them:

> I have never ever thought of repercussions. I don't believe if I do something the repercussion effect will be detrimental to me . . . I believe in fairness being continuous. If it does not resolve here, if he takes the next step and brings it back to me I will take the next step and take it further until we reach a platform. I am not frightened . . . My boss last year came to me and said 'you have a different personality'. I said 'I think we need personalities like mine in this world'. I have no idea how it came to me but it is with me . . . some people are so frightened of questioning because they think people will chop them down.

It is important to remember that self-efficacy is contextual; students might have a high sense of self-efficacy in terms of their ability to work on written assignments and a low sense of self-efficacy in terms of their ability to perform well in exams. Some students are highly successful in one area of their life, sport for example, where they demonstrate persistence, effort and perseverance, and yet they cannot apply these qualities to their studies. The contextual nature of self-efficacy beliefs helps us to understand this.

Self-concept

Another expectancy belief is self-concept. This differs from self-efficacy in that it is not so linked to context. Self-concept judgments can be domain-specific but are not task-specific, so in comparison to self-efficacy judgments they are more global. Included in a person's self-concept are feelings of self-worth associated with the behaviours in question. Thus, there is no fixed relationship between self-concept and self-efficacy. Students might have a high level of self-efficacy in relation to assessment items in a particular discipline, say science, but might not have a high self-concept in the same area. This can be partly due to the fact that they might not be proud of accomplishments in science; instead they might value accomplishment in another pursuit, for example, dramatic performance.

Self-efficacy and self-concept differ according to the source of an individual's judgment (Marsh *et al*. 1991). Marsh *et al*. suggest that a person makes external comparisons when making self-concept judgments, that they compare their self-perceptions of their own skills with the perceived skills of other students within their frame of reference (according to our data this would most likely be the students in a tutorial group, and perhaps any friends in other tutorial groups of the same course). They use this external relativistic impression as one basis for their self-concept in an area. Marsh *et al*. claim students also make an internal comparison when making judgments affected by self-concept, comparing one self-perceived skill against another. This internal, relativistic comparison is the second basis for their self-concept in an area.

In contrast with this comparison, factors that are important in the formation of self-concept beliefs may not play a major role in self-efficacy judgments, as the focus is on individuals' self-perception of their skills and capabilities. Self-efficacy judgments are based on an 'inferential process involving prior performance, vicarious experience, verbal persuasion, and emotional arousal' (Marsh *et al*. 1991: 335).

If it is accepted that self-concept is an expectancy belief that is measured at a broader level of specificity than self-efficacy, and domain- but not task-specific, we can see that the term applies to a student's broader sense of competence and self-worth. Students who generally feel competent and have a high sense of self-worth will view things differently than those who generally feel they lack competence and hold a low sense of self-worth. Students with a high self-concept will be more likely to approach teachers for feedback or clarification on issues and, if not resolved to their satisfaction, will be more likely to pursue the issues.

Jade appeared to be a student with a low self-concept. She failed three out of four courses in one study period yet did not seek feedback. In one case it was because she felt the person was not very approachable, but in the other two cases it was for a different reason:

> I felt really embarrassed about my grades and didn't want the lecturers to know that I was one of the people who failed their course. If I did that then they would probably recognize me in the future when I went back to repeat the course. I guess I also thought they probably wouldn't do anything about it anyway.
>
> (Jade, email)

Jade failed one of these courses a second time and felt it was unfair that she did not receive a conceded pass or a terminating pass because her other grades were a distinction, credit and P1, but again she did not do anything about it:

> I didn't approach the lecturer because I didn't want to be pinpointed . . . as one of the people that had failed it twice. He was very approachable

so that was never an issue. It was simply due to me feeling really dumb and embarrassed about it. I also knew that if I went to him he would go through my exam paper with me and show me all the stupid mistakes I made.

(Jade, email)

It appeared that in addition to having a low self-concept, Jade also lacked confidence and had a low sense of self-efficacy. She had enough self-efficacy to continue her commitment to achieving a university degree but certainly not to maximizing her opportunities for success.

Students' self-confidence, sense of self-efficacy and self-concept are modifiers that influence the response they have if they think they have been treated unfairly in assessment. Yet it is possible for teachers to influence students' sense of self (Dweck 2007). Students need to be taught that their intellectual ability is something they can develop through effort and education, and that their brain is capable of growth. Then teachers should give praise for engagement in the learning process (perseverance, strategies, improvement) rather than for 'intelligence'. This type of praise results in students gaining the requisite skills they need to maintain their confidence in learning; it allows them to see failure as an opportunity for growth. This has implications for the type of feedback students are given, particularly in their early years at university.

Students' perception of teachers' approachability

It was explained in the previous chapter that one of the key considerations a student takes into account when making a judgment of fairness about assessment is whether teachers display a caring attitude, and part of being caring is appearing approachable. Students' perception of whether teachers are approachable is also a response modifier that affects students' responses to unfair assessment. As Ian says, approachability '. . . would matter; if that person was more approachable then you would definitely feel more at ease going and asking what might have been required, or what I missed out on, what I didn't do'.

Unfortunately, some teachers appear intimidating to students. The lecturer Darren refers to in the excerpt below 'comes across as very angry'. While she appeared intimidating, she nevertheless helped him to understand a key concept:

I hadn't spoken to lecturer Z for a long time and one day I asked her a question and she sat me down and talked to me for a long time about it and it helped me out a lot. I didn't really take it all in properly and I came back and asked again. I thought I was going to get into trouble. She sat me down and took me through it again. When I said that to someone else and said 'Why don't you go and ask lecturer Z?' they said 'no way'. Lecturer Z comes across as very angry. No one really likes to talk to her. I didn't either until I actually spoke to her.

Darren believes that: 'Some lecturers make it hard for you though, but they don't know it; they're just not approachable.' We suspect that some teachers might be unaware that students view them as unapproachable. On the other hand, some cultivate a persona of not being approachable so that contact from students is lessened. Lecturer Z told us she likes it that students are scared of her as it gives her a greater sense of authority. Ironically, at the same time she did not believe students had issues related to fairness of assessment 'with her' because students 'do not bring such concerns to my attention'.

Ryan had a number of experiences that led him to believe that his teachers were not helpful because they 'thought they were better than the students'. He hesitated to ask for assistance or clarification on assessment matters that confused him. Ryan's experiences with a group of teachers who taught him in a series of elective courses was very different:

> In the X building every one of the lecturers, they're all over like fifty, sixty, they've been teaching for a while but they're the best lecturers you can have . . . They are so friendly over there. Like, you go into there and everyone is asking you 'What are you looking for? Can we help you?', that sort of thing . . . Even the students . . . the majority of people there know each other; they recognize each other's face . . . The lecturers there are always free, always got time for you, the most approachable people I have found at the school.

Because Ryan thought that the teachers in X building were approachable, he was confident to question and follow up any confusion he had about the course.

Students describe some teachers as genuinely approachable, while others seemed less genuine. Nathan describes the latter type as 'basically, they're just reading off a piece of paper to do what the [universities] ask. You know, you've got to be approachable, alright, we'll say we're approachable.' So Nathan's response to unfair assessment is dependent on his perception of the approachability of the teacher: 'If something is unfair I just let it slip sometimes. At other times, I ask and have a go at it. It depends, it depends on the actual lecturer, actually . . . If you've got a friendly lecturer . . .'

Nadia felt that prior involvement with teachers was an important factor influencing her willingness to approach them with an issue. If they had proven not to be helpful in another situation, she would not go to them again. Nadia commented that she felt she could speak with the programme director when she had an issue because: 'I knew her, and knew her face, had informal conversations with her before and felt I could speak with her about an issue.'

Students' knowledge of process

Knowledge of process refers to students' understanding of the options available to them if they perceive assessment to be unfair. This includes knowing what is contained in the university's *Assessment policies and procedures manual*. If students lack this specific knowledge, it can have major implications for their progress. For example, Gemma failed an assignment and approached the course coordinator to challenge her mark. The course coordinator did not follow due process and requested the original marker to re-mark it: there was no alteration of her mark. Gemma was not aware of university policy that a different person should have re-marked her work. This lack of knowledge of process limited Gemma's ability to take advantage of the university's policy on re-examination.

Georgia received a credit for an assignment but felt she deserved more. She did not think it was worth questioning because it was a minor assignment. Had she failed it, Georgia thought she would have asked her tutor or friends about what action she could take because, although she did not know what options were available to her, she knew there was 'some sort of process'. Georgia had heard of work being re-marked but was not aware that there was an official process for requesting a re-mark.

Knowledge of process is interrelated with other factors that influence student responses. For example, a student with a high level of desperation is more likely to find out what the processes are, for it is the desperation that prompts action to be taken. It is also possible that if a student knows what options are available to them, they might utilize those options in less extreme circumstances. These options include seeking clarification from teachers when unsure about criteria for assessment, asking a teacher to look over a draft of an essay, requesting clearer or more detailed feedback when receiving an assignment or making an appointment with the teacher following the release of the final grade of an examination.

Knowledge of process is also linked with students' perception of teachers' approachability. If the students perceive teachers to be approachable, and they know what their options are, they are more likely to raise and discuss issues with their teachers. Our data indicate that there is an exception to this. First, students might accept lower marks than they think they deserve and not question teachers because they like them and find them approachable. As Sammi says: 'Sometimes it will come down to that: a student will compromise his or her inner self to see that the relationship with the lecturer, if you can call it a relationship, is kept positive.' The irony is that the very fact the teacher is perceived as approachable means the students might be reluctant to question the teacher in case it damages the relationship they have with the teacher.

Interestingly, a greater number of the mature age students knew what options were available to them compared to the younger students. This is due to a range of reasons, including life experience (knowing that in most organizations there are processes of appeal); accepting greater responsibility for learning; and utilizing what the university offers, which includes consulting with teachers.

Students who have a sound knowledge of process understand the hierarchies in universities based on ascribed status and power. For example, they know very well that a tutor has less status and power than a lecturer, course coordinator, programme director and head of school. Knowing the hierarchy means knowing who to approach if there is an issue. Darren describes an incident when he failed a course in his first year, yet his classmates who usually received lower results than him passed. In retrospect he realized his failing grade was probably due to clerical error (his marks were recorded as 5 out of 100, so it appeared that some of his assignments had not been entered on the teacher's mark sheet). Initially Darren tried to contact the teacher to address the matter but gave up when he could not make contact. Unfortunately, his lack of knowledge of the system meant that he did not know whom to approach for assistance. Consequently, he failed the course and repeated it the following year.

Lack of knowledge of process would not prevent Nadia, in the fourth year of a double degree, from following up an issue. She said that if she did not know which individual to approach she would go to the student administration centre (the 'shopfront' in most universities for all matters relating to student life) 'and they would point me in the right direction'. She also said that she would seek advice from her tutor or course coordinator by email to find out how to have an assignment reassessed. While Nadia is not currently aware of all the specific processes that she could follow, she has broader help-seeking strategies in place.

Representing students' knowledge of process as a continuum helps make us aware of the range of student understanding of recourse opportunities when assessment is unfair. As shown in Figure 5.2, at one end of the continuum there are students who are clueless and, at the other end, knowledgeable.

It is only when students have an understanding of the processes of recourse that they are able to address unfair assessment. But whose responsibility is it that students develop a knowledge of process? Some students believe it is the responsibility of others to tell them what their options are. John, for example, suggests it is the fault of either the teacher or the lack of an informative orientation programme in first year that meant he did not realize he could apply for special consideration to re-sit an exam:

> I didn't pass the final exam. I did half of it and walked out because I just couldn't . . . the lecturer didn't ever say anything to me about me being given special consideration to re-sit the exam . . . I know we are supposed to know about it but back in our first year, you know how

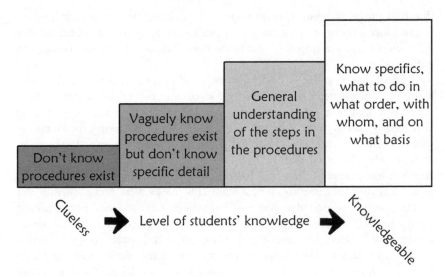

Figure 5.2 Students' knowledge of process

people have this orientation and all that kind of stuff? We had these like third years and all they did is say, there's the bar, and, there's the cafeteria, and that was it. That was my orientation.

Rosie thinks teachers are selective in what they tell students. For example, she says she has never been told that she can request a re-mark for an assignment:

They don't make it clear. I think we all in the back of our mind know that we could do something about it, but it is never clear. Like, they go through everything in the course outline, like for a week we go through it, but they never once say you can resubmit work for a complete, unbiased re-mark from someone else; they never ever say it. And I think if they did say it, it would probably make some people think, oh, maybe I could do something else . . . They need to make the processes more clear. Like, we all know we can go to Learning Connection [the section of the university that provides counselling, career, disability, and international student services] and we can go to the Head of School, but we don't know the direct, the small channels that we can take; the small channels are where we all struggle.

It is important to recognize that knowledge of process is a modifier that influences the response a student has when perceiving assessment to be unfair. Whose responsibility it is for the students to gain this knowledge is a separate issue but one that universities would be well advised to consider if they wish to reduce the frustration of students about assessment issues.

Response

Having explained that a series of response modifiers influences the response a student has to a perception of unfair assessment, we now discuss what the responses may be.

The real impact of a perception of unfair assessment is determined by what a student does or does not do. If students decide not to take any action, they are likely to miss opportunities to redress the unfairness. Students spoke very pragmatically of what they did if they perceived assessment to be unfair. We have categorized these into three groups of responses: taking action, opting out and surviving. These can be viewed as similar to three petals on a flower (see Figure 5.3).

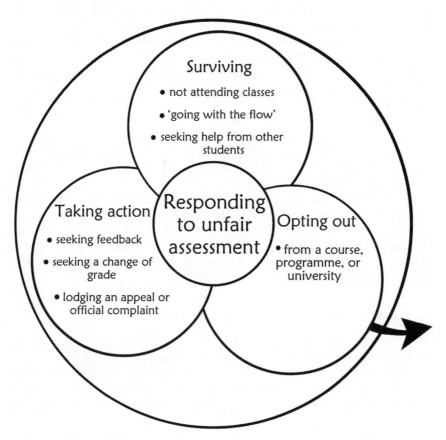

Figure 5.3 Stage two: Responding to unfair assessment. The responses

Taking action

We begin the discussion of the response 'taking action' by considering the words of Alise, reflecting on the first time she felt she had been treated unfairly: 'You may even be in a period of shock because you have never had to take action to do something . . . ooh, what's happening?'

The shock is common in first-year students – whose secondary schooling experiences are overwhelmingly positive – when they receive their first negative assessment at university. Although Alise spoke of being shocked, she nevertheless was committed to taking action to address what she thought was unfair assessment. In this way, making a judgment that assessment is unfair can have a positive outcome so long as students take action of some kind. An example of this is Allie. She presented as confident and determined about her post-university plans and was clear about the role of the university degree in helping her to achieve her career aspirations. Allie describes herself as a 'bit lazy; I don't study enough and I'm capable of achieving higher grades if I put in the effort'. Allie once received a low grade for an assignment. She thought that it was unfair as she usually got 'okay grades'. As it worried her for a long time, she eventually decided to speak to her teacher, who 'tore it apart, said I was lucky to get what I did'. Her initial reaction to this was disbelief about what the teacher had done. However, the critical feedback changed how she approached the next assignment because she now 'under-stood what the tutor wanted'. Allie's interpretation of the course booklet's instructions about how to write had not been correct. She thought she was doing what was expected, but once she spoke with the teacher she realized that she was not. Subsequently, if Allie has an issue she speaks with a teacher, 'except in minor cases where it isn't worth it', because the earlier experience of seeking feedback was beneficial.

Students who take action prepare themselves. They gather information, weigh up what to do based on possible consequences and usually ask advice from other students. Taking action can be viewed as on a range from informal through to formal – from seeking feedback or explanations, to seeking a change of grade or re-mark, to lodging an official appeal/complaint. We discuss each of these options in what follows.

Seeking feedback

Students seek feedback for various reasons. Most do not expect a change of grade but want to understand the reason they were awarded a particular mark. As Duncan explains, 'I'd go and see the lecturer and ask them why they thought it deserved that.' Many students are unsure about which sections of their assignments are satisfactory and which are unsatisfactory. As Steve says:

> You'd go to a lecturer and ask them to run through with you and explain what things you did wrong. Or rather, what they considered you did

wrong or you didn't include or, yeah, just missed the question. So, yeah, try and find out what you did wrong.

Melanie, while working on a group assignment, had approached a teacher to clarify the assessment criteria. The group followed the advice of the teacher and were shocked to receive a poor grade. These were high-achieving students in all other courses. Melanie questioned the teacher about why the group had received a poor mark: 'She pointed out why, but we were still annoyed. I didn't think that solved the problem.' Melanie's belief was that the teacher was unclear about what she wanted the students to do. Melanie said the criteria were ambiguous and able to be interpreted in many ways. There were legitimate grounds for objecting to the grade, but Melanie's group did not pursue the matter: 'there was nothing we could do, that's what she said so we have to go on what she said 'cause that's how she's marked it'. Melanie's group were not familiar with the university assessment policy – even if they were, it is possible that they would not have taken the matter further as they were being strategic in tolerating a short-term injustice in the interests of maintaining positive long-term relationships with their teacher. Such short-term acceptance of unfair assessment practices does not cause fundamental damage to the self-belief of high-achieving students. However, this is not always the case, particularly with students who are less successful.

We found that many students are confused about assessment criteria or the marks they receive, but only a few of them seek clarification. Many talk with other students but not the person who marks their work. Those who do approach teachers seeking feedback will avoid confrontational language by not saying to the teachers that they consider the mark to be unfair – even though this is often what they think, and it is often the motivation for approaching teachers. Darren, for example, does not find it easy to speak with teachers, but he knows that if a student does not talk about something that they think is unfair, the situation can get worse:

> For a lot of people it will get worse if they don't do anything when they think something is unfair. If something starts unfair then some people will just stop doing things; you just get lower and lower. It comes down to whether you talk to the lecturer enough.

So his advice is to 'talk to them and ask them why, how come I've been given this mark, I've put this much work in, the hours of work I've put in'.

Occasionally a student reported being quite assertive, such as Travis, who recounts a time that he received a mark that he thought was unfair:

> Yep, first thing I did was go in and see the lecturer and say 'I'm not used to getting this. I don't expect you to change my grade to a distinction or anything, but I just want to know how I can do better

because obviously I don't want to get a result like this next time because I got a P1'.

Most students, however, exercise a level of subtlety in their approach, as these examples show:

> I'd have to sort it out if I thought something was marked unfairly. I'd have to go and ask why, where did I go wrong, what do I need to improve on? . . . I would go to the person who's marked it and say, 'Look what's the story here, what happened?' But in a non-aggressive manner.
>
> (Ginny)

> It doesn't have to be very drastic, questioning a lecturer. It can be informal.
>
> (Sammi)

Some students made it clear that they did not want to be seen as simply 'complaining' or 'whinging' about their assessment. They were more interested in receiving feedback that would allow them to improve in future assessment tasks. As Ursula and Victor explain:

> . . . not for whinging, or anything, just for feedback. I mean, hey, you know, you can't expect to get – I mean I don't get HDs all the time by any means, but, yeah, some things, you're going to do better at other things, so you just accept, ask and if that's the way it is, then that's the way it is. Yeah, I don't whinge about everything.
>
> (Ursula)

> I might go to a lecturer and say . . . I didn't do very well in my last assignment and I'm not sure why. She said, because of this here. I don't go complaining that I should have got a better mark because it's just not going to happen. It's like complaining to an umpire in sport. They're not going to change their decision. You've just got to work out what you did wrong and why, so you don't do it next time.
>
> (Victor)

Examples were given earlier in the chapter about students advising or counselling others to speak with teachers. Both of the students giving advice were mature age students – they play an important role in educating the younger students about the circumstances in which it is appropriate to question their teachers. Samantha speaks of acting like a mediator for other students, not in the sense of approaching teachers on their behalf, but rather to help them work out whether seeking feedback is a valid action:

But I've also had a few students who have come up to me and their work looks pretty good, and I've said to them, if I were you I would at least ask, there's not a problem in asking, go and approach them and say, 'Look, this is what I've done, this is what you've asked me to do, I don't think I've missed anything, could you give me a bit more feedback on where I've gone wrong'. So, I have been approached by other students to do that kind of thing, sort of act as a mediator almost.

There is some commonality between the positive results of students who take action – specifically, seeking feedback – when they perceive assessment to be unfair and the positive results of people who use an enactment perspective in crisis situations. 'Enactment' is a term used to show that when people act they bring events and structures into existence and set them in motion (Weick 1988). In situations where people use an enactment perspective, Weick suggests that they 'could think about crises in ways that highlight their own actions and decisions as determinants of the conditions they want to prevent' (1988: 316).

We are not claiming that perceptions of unfairness are in the same league as crises such as gas leaks, radioactive leaks or space shuttle crashes, to which Weick is referring. However, students who think about unfairness in assessment in ways that highlight their own actions and decisions can prevent further situations in which they feel they lack control, become demoralized and feel as if the system has let them down. By taking action they are likely to improve the situation for themselves.

Borrowing from Weick's (1988) enactment perspective, and applying it to our data, we can see that there are four implications for students who seek feedback. These are part of a 'feedback-seeking cycle'. First, by seeking feedback, students' perceptions of control increase and their stress decreases. As their stress decreases they are able to view the situation with greater perspective, which in turn increases their perception of control. Second, by receiving feedback, students can often transform a more complex task into a simpler task – receiving feedback clarifies what the problem is and consolidates an otherwise confusing set of information. The simplification of the problem results in a further decrease in stress. Third, by receiving feedback and making necessary changes the mistakes or bad habits or misunderstandings might not be repeated in other assignments. This prevents the downward spiralling effect that some students report when they perceive assessment to be unfair. Finally, perhaps the most important implication for students who seek feedback is that it gives them a better appreciation of how they can take control of their learning, and of how they are responsible for their own learning.

Students we interviewed who received outstanding grades were more likely to take action and have greater control over their learning. A study by Nesbit and Burton (2006) shows that students who received credit and distinction grades and who thought that the assessment process was unfair did not have low self-efficacy or reduced motivation. Yet students with pass grades and perceptions of unfairness had low satisfaction, low self-efficacy and decreased expectations of future performance. Our results suggest that higher achieving students are more likely to seek extra feedback, therefore increasing their self-efficacy.

Seeking a change of grade

Another way of taking action is to seek a change of grade. Rosie was a member of a tutorial group that received results that were consistently one or two grades lower than another group. She spoke with her tutor, despite the fact that many students would not approach the tutor as, 'she is really confronting, this lady, no one likes doing one-on-one with her because she just gets . . . it's your own fault you didn't do so well.' As Rosie was unhappy with the outcome of the meeting she contacted the course coordinator, who was also the tutor of the group receiving higher marks. He refused to intervene in the case. After the course was over, Rosie and a few other students met with the programme director and expressed their dissatisfaction with the performance of the tutor. Rosie said she would have requested an official re-mark of the assignment had she known it was possible. None of the staff members she approached had mentioned this as an option. Rosie continued to be angry about this experience because she had been incorrectly told nothing could be done.

Some students will approach a teacher seeking a change of grade if they are confident that their work should have received a higher grade. The following comments illustrate some of the different ways students approach teachers. Samantha showed how prepared she was for a meeting by explaining the connection between the assessment criteria and how she had addressed them:

> Each time I've – and I've only done it twice in my whole three years – I've questioned the grade that I've got but each time I've gone back to the criteria and I've actually detailed what I've done with the criteria and the points that I thought that I had missed. And I've asked the lecturer, 'Look, this is your criteria, this is what I've done, this is how I've responded to that. Admittedly I may have missed your point, however – .' And I've actually used that as supporting evidence for my argument. So, one time it worked, the other time it didn't.

Like Samantha, Sammi prepared himself well:

> When we got an unfair group mark I practically ran back to read regulations in the assessment policies and procedures manual, then had a session with our international student advisor. I just wanted to know

what the regulations were, so I said 'explain to me if this thing happens, what can I do?' I wanted to be informed before I did anything, or made my decision, or whatever. I needed to be informed of things first.

As a result of this preparation, Sammi asked his teacher to reconsider the distribution of the grades given to the whole class for a group assignment, not just his own:

Her question to me was 'What do you want? Do you want a HD or a D?' I said 'No, I don't want a D or an HD, I want fair assessment, that is what I want. If you are going to reassess mine please grade the rest, don't just grade mine' . . . and she did. She increased a few others who were in the same category.

Louise was not so calm about her issue:

This guy was really unfair, but there was an issue here and I was really cross about it; I'm really headstrong. That low mark obviously needed to be resolved, otherwise it would have gone on, and it was resolved there and then by approaching the lecturer and it didn't happen again. Where I think if I had let it go it probably would have affected my whole entire marks for that course. I actually had him again two years later by accident and he was really good. I think if I hadn't resolved it there and then it would have continued and then I would have been penalized two years on.

Interestingly, Louise's perception that dealing with the issues meant the teacher did not penalize her later is the opposite view to that held by many students who worry that approaching teachers with an issue will have a negative impact on them. This was discussed earlier in the chapter under the response modifier 'concern about ramifications'.

Amy met with her teacher and negotiated a change of grade, but if that had not been the outcome she probably would not have pursued the matter further: 'If I had received an unsatisfactory hearing I probably wouldn't have done anything. It's too hard and time consuming chasing up things like that' (Amy, email). Amy's acceptance that she would not do anything further – had the hearing been unsatisfactory – is not uncommon. Many students who perceive assessment to be unfair will not take action at an official level because to them this represents an intolerable escalation of the problem.

Lodging an appeal or official complaint

Only a few students spoke of lodging an appeal against a decision or formalizing a complaint. There are two response modifiers that have the greatest influence on students' reluctance to complain: their level of desperation and their concerns about the negative ramifications if they complain. It is only when they are really angry or annoyed, or when they have few other options, that they take what they perceive to be 'drastic action'.

Students are at times very dissatisfied with the attitude, approach or behaviour of their teachers and are clearly very upset by some of their experiences. They talk about being 'annoyed', 'angry', 'frustrated', 'resentful', 'totally pissed off', 'cross', 'disgruntled', 'cheated', 'duped' and 'defensive'.

Sammi found that lodging an official complaint was very difficult. He spoke of an incident in his home country where he went to the programme director after he failed to resolve a disputed mark with his lecturer:

> It is really a difficult process. I am a mature student and I still – when I received the low mark this time around – I think reacted much better than the last time when I was back in my home country. The last time I was really vocal and a little bit arrogant in my approach to getting it resolved. I left the lecturer and I went right to the program director and requested an audience and we came back and had a meeting . . . Maybe because of my involvement in unionism – at that time I was also the president of the student council – so I was used to taking grievances to the top . . . Also the lecturer, to me, was not professional. The issue was dealing with his professionalism and because he wasn't professional I felt I had to take it to the next step.

Sammi made an official complaint because he thought his teacher lacked professionalism.

However, it is beyond the realm of possibility for many students that they will engage in the level of challenge for which Sammi was prepared. Only one other student, Louise, was prepared to take this kind of formal action. She spoke to her head of school after a teacher did not make changes to grades that she felt were unfairly assigned. The result of the conversation with the head of school was that grades were changed for a number of students.

Some students planned to complain formally at the end of a teaching period but frequently did not follow through. For some, this is because they believed that it would be a waste of time and nothing would change. Other students were relieved their contact with the teacher was over:

> I had just had enough of that guy by the end of the course . . . so had everyone else. I just said to them, 'Look, if you want I will put a letter together and everyone can sign it'. By the end of semester everyone is just going, 'It's over. We're never having him again. It doesn't matter.'
> (Veronica)

Despite students being quite dissatisfied with the attitude, approach or behaviour of teachers most students chose not to use official ways of complaining of these issues. Formalizing an issue of concern more often follows dissatisfaction with a grade than dissatisfaction with other aspects of assessment (such as lack of feedback, teachers perceived as not caring, lack of perceived relevance of assessment items). This is not surprising as university appeals systems relating to assessment usually focus on the determination of grades. When students are dissatisfied with a grade they sometimes investigate what the process of appeal entails and often find it too daunting to proceed, and so they make a decision that the possible outcome is not worth the time and effort.

Opting out

We now turn to the second group of responses common to students who perceive assessment as unfair. 'Opting out' refers to the behaviour of students who decide not to continue in a course, programme or the university because they feel they have no choice but to withdraw.

While we know the numbers of students who withdraw from their university studies, we are less clear about the reasons for their decisions. However, from our study we know many students opt out because they perceive assessment to be unfair. In this way, assessment practices are strongly implicated in increasing attrition rates in our universities.

We spoke with a number of students who opted out of a course and, in the case of a *core* course, chose to repeat it later in the hope of getting a different teacher. Ursula seriously considered dropping out of a course but managed to complete it. She speaks about this incident with a sense of relief:

> I don't want to give up, because I'm doing this for myself, but thinking that my assessment was unfair made me consider dropping out of the course and picking it up the next year, because I was really struggling with it, because nothing was making sense ... Yeah, I think being treated unfairly would, it would give someone the motivation to pull out, yeah.

Not all students have the same success as Ursula. Nerilee came across – quite independently of each other – two students who had studied in one of the programmes from which the students for the study were sourced. In general conversation with each one, she asked why they had not completed their degree, and each spoke about leaving university one core course short of completion. They were avoiding a teacher who had a reputation among the students for high failure rates in the core course, and whom they felt disliked them. The two students were so sure that they would fail, they planned to return when the teacher retired, which at that time they thought was imminent. Whether they would have failed or not we cannot know, but such is the power of their perception that they took such extreme action. What they had not accounted for was the number of years before the teacher did retire, and consequently neither student returned to university to complete their degree.

In our research, we conducted interviews with students who were currently at university, and therefore it should be noted that we did not speak with students who had opted out of university, apart from the two mentioned above.

Among our interviewees, Nathan had considered leaving university: 'Yes, without a doubt ... I've thought about leaving uni because I was being treated unfairly ... but I stayed because I think I'm better than this. I can do it.' He says he does know of other students who have left because they thought the way that their teacher presented their course was unfair; according to Nathan, the teacher refused to help students when they were experiencing problems:

> A few people have left, just because of 'course X'. They just didn't get enough help. They were just scared. 'I'm going to be coming back and I'm going to be doing the same course again. I just can't cope with that. I'm going to go and do TAFE [technical and further education].'

Darren also knows students who have left the programme: 'If something is unfair it can just get bigger than what it is without anything happening. Yeah, students can leave the programme over it.' Travis provides a similar report:

> It would probably be enough for them to sort of pack their bags and it could well be, depending on how unfair it was, I mean, what experience they've had ... If it disturbed you in such a way that you thought, 'Hey, this is just not worth it. I'm not getting anything out of this. This is too unfair' and out the door. And I know a lot of people have done that. They've probably thought, well, this is not the right programme for me.

Most students have a response to a perception of unfairness of assessment that is not as extreme as opting out, and not as resolute as taking action. We turn to these next.

Surviving

Surviving is a relatively passive response to dealing with a perception of unfair assessment, but it means students are still engaged in the process of demonstrating capability. A surviving response enables students to endure a situation in the short term but not experience the benefits of engaging in full university life.

The surviving response is similar to opting out; the students do not leave but do not fully participate in their learning programme. Most students who use a surviving response do not interact with teachers; in many cases, students actively avoid them. A student may have initially sought help, but after not getting a resolution that is satisfactory to them, they adopt the surviving response. We have identified three surviving responses:

- not attending classes
- 'going with the flow'
- seeking help from other students.

Not attending classes

A number of students reported not attending tutorials or lectures if they perceived assessment to be unfair. For example, Rosie thought her teacher did not care about her; in fact, she believed she was being persecuted:

> You make an excuse, like they have a thing for me, they hate me . . . Lecturer X probably didn't hate me, for all I know, but I felt like I was getting persecuted every time because I had that mentality. So I thought, I don't want to be here anymore, I'm not going to come. If I come and I see that you are going to be foul, I won't go in.

Rosie's response was not to attend classes. She acknowledges in retrospect that she probably had a particular 'head-set' about the teacher and that the feeling of persecution can be 'all in your mind'. However, at the time it was her 'individual reality' (Schein 1992), and by not attending classes she was able to cope.

John did not attend specific lectures but for a very different reason. He did not believe the lecturer treated the female students with as much respect as the male students – they were not operating on a level playing field:

> I had seen the way lecturer X was speaking to the girls and it disgusts me. I couldn't, I will not take lectures from a man that treats his students like that . . . I think he is a dickhead so I didn't go to his lectures, but I would see the course outline to see when lecturer Y was teaching and that is when I would turn up.

By not attending the lectures given by lecturer X, John felt he was able to continue in the course. John adopted the strategy of not attending on another occasion when he was repeating a course that he had failed. He had been unsuccessful in appealing the fail and felt that he was going to be victimized: 'If you've got "bad blood" with the lecturer the second time round you are not going to want to be there . . . not going to class helps me cope.' By getting the lecture notes from a friend, John was able to avoid the lecturer and managed to pass the course.

Gemma was convinced a teacher did not like her because she had not attended optional tutorials. She was also convinced that the teacher had failed her in an assignment because she did not like her. Gemma felt she had done well in the assignment so went to the course coordinator, who had asked the teacher to re-mark the assignment. Gemma in her email interview said:

> She did re-mark it but gave me 49% failing me by one percent! u bet I wasn't angry! then I just decided to let it go it was too much of a hassle and because I held a grudge against the teacher I did not attend any more tutes for the rest of the semester and ended up failing the course!

While Gemma believes her problem began by not attending tutorials, her solution was to stop attending all classes. In Gemma's case, this survival response was counterproductive in that she failed the course.

'Going with the flow'

'Going with the flow' describes the surviving response of students who do nothing in response to a perception of unfair assessment. They do not take action of any sort; they just continue doing what they were doing. It is not surprising that many students do not question or challenge teachers when we reflect on some of their descriptors of how they feel when they think assessment is unfair: 'bemused', 'dejected', 'knocks confidence', 'reduces confidence', 'erodes confidence', 'system against you', 'lacking control', 'victim', 'very uncomfortable', 'pull back', 'self-doubt', 'disheartened', 'knocked back', 'demoralizing', 'upset', 'confused', 'shock', 'bewilderment', 'sad', 'lose interest', 'useless', 'drag your feet' and 'disappointed'. As Nadine said, 'Yes, sometimes you just wear it, sometimes you think that the recourse is going to cause more trouble than fixing the issue.'

Some students report that their response is to accept failure, knowing they will repeat the course. Some express hope for a different teacher when they repeat, but others do not think as proactively as this.

We used the example earlier of Darren, who had failed a course in his first year, probably due to a clerical error. He had attempted to get an answer about why he had failed but gave up. He repeated the course without attending many sessions and received a credit. His survival mechanism was to accept failure and repeat. Two years later he is still confused over what happened – it was the only course he failed at university.

Gemma, the student mentioned above who unsuccessfully tried the strategy of not attending classes, had a different response the second time round, when repeating the course. This time she became quite ill and was granted extensions for all of her assignments:

When the [extended] due dates came around I still had not recovered from the illness so my effort would have been the same as if I had done it by the actual due dates. I did not speak to staff about my problems as I was at home all the time; I just emailed explaining my situation and hoped I would get better. I felt it was too much hassle to keep putting things off so I just did them and prayed that I would pass.

Gemma did not pass, did not apply for special consideration, accepted failure and knew she would begin again the next year. The strategy of accepting failure and repeating did not work, as she failed again. Finally, in her third attempt at the course, Gemma decided to put in more effort from the beginning:

I am coping well with the course. At the moment I am finding it very easy as I already know what we are learning so it is more a memory refresher rather than learning anything new. I am doing it differently this semester. I am attending all tutes and lectures, and doing my tute work each week, unlike last time I did it when I did not put in much effort ... Failing has made me try harder definitely as I don't have an interest in [course name] and I definitely don't want to do it for a fourth time!
(email interview)

Had Gemma miraculously passed the first time when she had hardly attended class, or the second time when she had applied for extensions and prayed that she would pass, she might not have altered her approach to study. Hopefully, Gemma's increase in attendance and application in the third attempt will transfer to her approach in other courses. Gemma's perception of unfairness was probably not well-founded in the first place – but she managed to stay in the system and ultimately succeed. Accepting failure and repeating is not necessarily a retrograde response, as long as the student institutes some change in behaviour when repeating. Meeting with students who have failed a course and getting them to articulate what changes they will make may be useful in assisting them to succeed when repeating a course.

While writing this book we also met a part-time mature age student who was in the final year of completing a second undergraduate degree. In her second year she was concerned about marks she received for a course and initially questioned the teacher. She was so disgruntled with the answer from the teacher that she adopted a surviving response of not collecting her assignments after they had been graded. She no longer pays any attention to her grades or feedback. She says it causes her far less angst.

Seeking help from other students

The final survival response, of seeking help from other students, is similar to the 'taking action' group of responses. However, we place it in this grouping because it does not involve interacting with teachers. Students who use this strategy find ways to cope with perceptions of unfairness in assessment by turning to their peers for help. Students talk with other students specifically to find out how they can improve their work, rather than asking teachers for feedback.

Students also seek help from their peers over issues other than unfair grades. For example, Nathan had completely 'given up on' his teacher, who in his view was incapable of teaching the content of the course and had been belittling him in class when he asked questions. Nathan was studying a core course that he needed to pass to stay in the degree. His response was to turn to the other students who had more experience with some of the underlying concepts associated with the course. By not speaking to the teacher – who was doing nothing for his self-confidence – and instead getting help from his peers, Nathan was able to pass the course. Nathan continued to attend class but relied on his peers after each session to clarify what had been presented.

Variation of responses and how they feed back into the process of demonstrating capability

As explained at the beginning of the chapter, the response students have to a perception of unfairness of assessment varies, depending on the response modifiers present. The response of students will not necessarily be the same at any one point in time for two different assessment items. For example, if students think that assessment is unfair, and perceive the teacher to be approachable, they might seek an explanation or extra feedback from the teacher. The same students making a similar judgment with an assessment item in another course, but with a teacher they perceive as not approachable, might not seek an explanation or extra feedback – instead they might feel mistreated and complain to their friends. In each case the students judged assessment to be unfair but in one situation sought feedback and in the other complained to friends.

The feedback-seeking cycle, described earlier in the chapter, showed that the response might not be the same in subsequent situations because the results of seeking feedback, or not seeking feedback, will have influenced the students in some way. If students' experiences of seeking feedback are positive, they are likely to develop the confidence to speak with teachers they perceive to be unapproachable. Perhaps they will view a similar situation differently, so the next time they will not perceive the assessment incident as unfair. Or perhaps the experience of seeking feedback will not have a positive outcome, and the next time they will respond to a judgment of unfairness by opting out. This scenario is less likely but not improbable – some students did report very unsatisfactory outcomes when seeking feedback.

Complaining to friends and feeling mistreated, and not seeking feedback, results in other possibilities. The act of complaining and feeling mistreated might result in students further inflaming their emotional reactions, and further decreasing both their sense of self-efficacy and belief that change can happen.

Another example is that students might adopt one of the surviving strategies listed, such as not attending class. The next time a similar situation arises they might opt out of the course, programme or university, or they might take action. It will depend on the response modifiers, and the result of the previous experience, particularly whether they passed the course or whether they failed. The experience the students had the first time, when they chose to attend fewer classes, might mean they revise or change the key considerations they take into account when making a fairness judgment in future courses. For example, they might not expect the teachers to be as caring, perhaps even accepting more responsibility for their own learning. The result of not attending classes might result in the response modifiers changing – they might have less concern about ramifications and decide that teachers do not need to appear approachable for them to seek assistance.

Whatever the response of students to a judgment of unfairness in assessment, the outcome of that response will feed back into the cycle of demonstrating capability. It might alter how students make their next fairness judgment about assessment, their emotional reaction or their response modifiers.

Conclusion

We have shown, in this second stage of the process of demonstrating capability, that students respond to unfair assessment in various ways; apart from the emotional reaction they have, they might take action, opt out or merely survive. We have also described the six modifiers that influence students' responses to unfair assessment: level of desperation, concern about ramifications, maturity, self-beliefs, perception of teachers' approachability and knowledge of process. These modifiers change over time, and indeed, part of the impetus for them changing is the outcome of the response.

As detailed at the end of the chapter, the process of demonstrating capability is cyclical. The outcome of the response, in addition to influencing the response modifiers, also influences the students' future emotional reaction – as well as having an impact on subsequent fairness judgments they make about assessment.

In the next, and final, chapter we summarize the key findings presented in earlier chapters and explore their implications for teachers, course coordinators, programme teams and university policy developers. We present numerous practical recommendations to increase students' and teachers' understanding of assessment issues and to promote the adoption of assessment policies and practices that are fair and equitable.

Chapter 6

Making assessment fairer

> The assessment of students is a serious and often tragic enterprise. Less pomposity and defensiveness and more levity about the whole business would be an excellent starting point for improving the process of evaluating and judging our students' learning.
>
> (Ramsden 2003: 176)

Students apply diverse criteria to decide whether assessment arrangements are fair or unfair. Students also have choices about what to do if they think they are being treated unfairly. But is it their sole responsibility to respond, or do their teachers have some moral duty to assist them in these situations? Should teachers leave it up to the students' own devices or should they help? If they decide to help, there is much they can do. In this chapter we present recommendations for course coordinators, teachers, programme teams and universities who want to promote fair assessment: assessment that gives students the opportunity to demonstrate their capability, and to have that capability recognized.

We begin by summarizing our findings. We also include recommendations for further research.

Insights into students' views on assessment

It is impossible to have a system of assessment that every student will perceive to be fair all of the time. The theory of demonstrating capability has shown that students have different experiences of assessment, perceive fairness differently, and respond in different ways when they perceive unfairness.

As we have explained in this book:

1   Students have varied understandings of the fairness of assessment based on different constructions of what constitutes a 'level playing field'.
2   Students judge the fairness of assessment by much more than the grade awarded for an assessment item. They take into account such things as the nature and extent of feedback they receive, the quality of their teachers, and the balance, variety and relevance of assessment tasks.

3   Positive relationships between teachers and students are important for many students, including the need for teachers to display a caring attitude.
4   Many students do not accept full responsibility for their learning; they frequently rely on teachers to motivate them, and shift the blame for their poor performance from themselves to their teachers.
5   Students can have a more positive experience at university if they are knowledgeable about assessment policies, and are prepared to act if they think that they have been treated unfairly.

While many of the recommendations that follow involve refining or changing assessment practices, findings 3 and 4 above require change to be at the deepest cultural level, the level of assumptions.

Some things are easy to change once teachers are aware of their impact on students. For example, it is relatively simple to change the balance of assessment tasks, or to provide detailed and consistent information about assessment tasks to all students. However, some aspects of assessment arrangements are difficult to change as they are deeply embedded within the culture of the university. For example, the relative power differentials between teachers and students are difficult to disrupt. This means that many students, because of their positioning, are unlikely to challenge teachers about assessment decisions. Attempts to empower students within such unequal power relations will not be easy.

The theory of demonstrating capability shows that students who engage in learning and are proactive in their approach to assessment are more able to resolve the problem of frustration with assessment. Students who accept responsibility for their learning are advantaged in that they achieve educational outcomes that meet their expectations, and their educational experience is positive. For the majority of students to accept responsibility, rather than a few, a change in assumptions needs to occur. We cannot expect students to enter the university and immediately operate as self-directed learners as a result of enrolling in a programme.

Recommendations

Having generated a theory, we now turn to what it means for universities and what it means for university teachers.

In Australia, national newspapers report rankings of teaching performance of publicly funded universities. Despite the controversy related to the methodology used to arrive at the results, results for low-ranking universities are not well received by their vice-chancellors. One positive outcome of the publication of rankings is that universities now take assessment practices more seriously, for assessment practices are one of the areas of most concern to students.

The following are suggestions for course coordinators, teachers, programme teams and the university.

Course coordinators

The following recommendations are relevant to course coordinators because they have responsibility for designing assessment items and writing course booklets:

1   Conveying expectations
2   Variety and balance of assessment items
3   Exams
4   Group work
5   Relevance to generic skills
6   Relevance to careers
7   Empowerment of students.

1 Conveying expectations

As we have said throughout the book, students need to know and understand what their teachers expect them to do in assessment tasks, and what criteria and standards their teachers use to judge the quality of their performances. Examples of both excellent and poor assignment and exam answers can help set expectations (Nesbit and Burton 2006), as can specific information about the number of references expected, presentation standards, word count and granting of extensions.

2 Variety and balance of assessment items

Course coordinators should ensure that a variety of assessment tasks are included in a course. Similarly, no single item should be weighted too heavily as some students can be seriously disadvantaged because unbalanced assessment arrangements prevent them from demonstrating their capability. Dunn *et al.* (2004) suggest many ways of adapting traditional assessment practices.

3 Exams

If course coordinators are going to include examinations in their assessment package, they should consider what it is they really want to test. Open-book exams reduce students' anxiety, can test higher-order thinking and problem solving and allow for the critical evaluation of key concepts rather relying on, and rewarding, rote memorization. Unless speed is an assessment criterion, students should be allowed ample time to complete exams. Again, this will lessen anxiety and increase the opportunity for students to demonstrate what they know. There are many texts available that provide information about exams (for example, Brown and Knight 1994; Miller *et al.* 1998; Race and Brown 1998; Race *et al.* 2005).

4 Group work

Course coordinators should ensure that the purpose of group work matches the assessment task and criteria (Webb 1995). Group selection processes also require careful consideration (for a summary, see Blowers 2006). There is merit in Blowers' (2006) proposition of grouping students according to a self-assessment of their skills, so that groups are formed with members holding a variety of skills – obviously this needs to match the purpose of the assessment. It is also important that students are provided with an avenue to give anonymous feedback regarding the functioning of their group. Finally, course coordinators should consider allocating marks for group processes as well as for the outcome of the group assessment.

5 Relevance to generic skills

Perceived relevance of assessment tasks is critical to students. However, emphasizing the generic skills used in assessment tasks can expand students' views of what is relevant in assessment. These are attributes, or qualities, loosely grouped around scholarship, global citizenship and lifelong learning. Examples of attributes are the ability to work collaboratively, having effective problem-solving skills, being committed to ethical action and social responsibility, being attuned to cultural diversity, and having a set of flexible and transferable skills for different types of employment.

6 Relevance to careers

Often students have very narrow understandings of what is relevant to their future careers. Course coordinators should make explicit links between the assessment tasks they set and their relevance to future workplaces.

7 Empowerment of students

Teachers can directly influence some of the modifiers that prevent students from taking action when they perceive assessment to be unfair. An example of a response modifier is students' lack of knowledge of process. Knowledge of process refers to students' understanding of the options available to them if they perceive assessment to be unfair. Course coordinators should explicitly educate students about the assessment policies and procedures that exist in the university. While this does not directly deal with the reluctance of many students to question teachers, it would help many students if they were informed of what their options are if they believe that assessment is unfair, including whether they can request a re-mark of an assignment. This requires an understanding of the hierarchy within academic and administrative appointments in universities. This hierarchy may seem logical to academics, but to many students it is confusing. Course coordinators should consider informing students about the different roles and responsibilities associated with various positions. This information could be included in course booklets.

Teachers

Teachers play extremely powerful roles in the assessment process. Ursula reinforces this when she comments on something her lecturer said in the first week in a course: 'He just told us that he doesn't give out high distinctions. You know, we're not worthy. I mean, how unfair is that?' Since students are focused on demonstrating their capabilities, how unfair it must seem to have a teacher make a pre-emptive judgment about the range of assessment grades he would apply without even seeing any student work. This reinforces the powerful position that teachers occupy:

1 Dealing with perceptions
2 Negotiating assessment
3 Establishing expectations
4 Explaining course booklets
5 Engaging in self-reflection
6 Involving students in the assessment process
7 Sharing information consistently
8 Problematizing assessment
9 Awarding grades and providing feedback
10 Showing you care
11 Supporting students to take action
12 Being available for students.

1 Dealing with perceptions

The theory of demonstrating capability deals with perceptions. One approach to addressing the issues this study has raised is to alter students' perceptions and expectations – this is particularly pertinent in cases where their perceptions are based on a lack of information, incorrect information or unrealistic expectations of their teachers. Students should accept responsibility for their learning, and part of this may involve knowing more about the assessment process.

2 Negotiating assessment

Some teachers push the 'boundaries of academic assessment discourse' by empowering learners to design their own assessment, choose and/or negotiate criteria, and have the opportunity to assess their own work (Leach *et al.* 2001: 303). While many teachers will not empower students to this degree, we think that students should be more involved in assessment processes than they are currently.

Empowering students does not mean they should expect to do less work, that the quality of work will be lower, that assessment will be easier or that standards will drop. It does mean students will engage more with their learning.

3 Establishing expectations

To some degree, the teachers in a university help to mould the expectations of the students. For example, if the majority of teachers are perceived to be approachable, course booklets are detailed with clear assessment criteria, and comprehensive feedback is given on assignments, those become the norm. Teachers not complying with the norm will be perceived by students as unfair – either because of their actions, teaching approach or assessment practice.

It is important to work out which student expectations are realistic, sustainable and educationally sound. A relatively recent example of a change in expectations is students' demand for online lecture notes. With the advent of PowerPoint presentations and course homepages on university websites, students find it hard to understand why some teachers do not provide notes. The teachers who choose not to provide notes are faced with an increasingly antagonistic audience of students. We are not suggesting that teachers should provide lecture notes, but rather that they will need to explain their pedagogical reasons for not providing them.

4 Explaining course booklets

Many of the frustrations students experience would be reduced if teachers provided full explanations of the information contained in the detailed course booklets. This might involve examining specific mark-sheets associated with each assessment item and explaining in detail how to request extensions, what the word count actually means, and what consequences are associated with late submissions.

5 Engaging in self-reflection

In addition to providing students with detailed course booklets, there needs to be a clearer focus on what are often unstated expectations. For example, course booklets rarely state explicit expectations about grammar, punctuation styles and other language conventions, but most university teachers tacitly apply those criteria when assessing a piece of written work. Similarly, students giving oral presentations may be judged negatively if their style of dress does not conform to their teachers' tacit expectations of how they should dress.

The very fact that the expectations are tacit makes them problematic, for even the teachers may not be aware of them. Schön (1983, 1987, 1991) recommends that all teachers engage in reflective practice, 'reflection-in-action' (thinking what they are doing when they are doing it) and 'reflection-on-action' (conscious reflection after the event), which would make teachers' taken-for-granted expectations more explicit and public.

6 Involving students in the assessment process

Students need to understand more about the assessment process than they do currently. They need to appreciate the nuances of assessment. Teachers are in an ideal position to initiate this understanding, to challenge students' taken-for-granted assumptions about assessment, to teach students about the complexities of assessment. For example, it would be useful for teachers to acknowledge that assessment and marking is, to a degree, subjective (Fleming 1999; Bloxham and West 2004). Involving students in peer assessment exercises would enable them to realize the difficulty of marking consistently against some criteria. Peer assessment also has the potential for many other benefits to students. Falchikov's (2005, 2007) work provides a great entrée into this field, showing that peer assessment is much more than students awarding grades to each other.

Various forms of peer assessment can enhance the quality of group work (Gatfield 1999; Walker 2001; Divaharan and Atputhasamy 2002; Freeman and McKenzie 2002; Gupta 2004), although not all researchers have this view (White *et al.* 2005). Some have noted that peer assessment produces a new range of problems, including inconsistent judgments by students and personal conflicts (Kennedy 2005). However, Falkichov (2007) suggests that training students in the peer assessment process leads to positive learning outcomes.

Self-assessment activities, where students apply assessment criteria to their own work, can be instrumental in promoting a greater acceptance of responsibility in students (Williams 1992; Sambell and McDowell 1997), and can also be effective in increasing students' understanding of assessment. An intervention programme with students run by Rust *et al.* (2003) is an example worth considering. Its aim was to increase knowledge of assessment criteria and processes by involving students in completing a mark-sheet for two sample assignments. Students then participated in a workshop with a structured analysis of the mark-sheets and the students' work. Three weeks later they submitted their assignments with a completed self-assessment sheet. By undertaking these self-assessment tasks students were able to understand more fully the tacit aspects of the assessment criteria and thus improve their performance. A resource leaflet outlining this intervention programme, along with much other excellent information about assessment and feedback, is on the website of the Assessment Standards Knowledge exchange (ASKe), the Centre of Excellence for Teaching and Learning based at Oxford Brookes University Business School.

An added benefit of the intervention programme suggested by Rust and his colleagues is that students come to realize that complete consistency and objectivity in marking is not always possible, despite the best intentions of the marker.

7 Sharing information consistently

Teachers should be aware that they may advantage some students over others when they share assessment information inconsistently – and that many students perceive this to be unfair. The following are strategies that require little input of time and effort but can enhance perceptions of equity about the distribution of information: utilizing time in lectures to clarify key issues, sending out class email answers to questions asked by students, establishing online resources for disseminating information to avoid disadvantaging part-time students or students who cannot attend campus easily, staying after class for a few minutes or getting to class ten minutes early. While the meaning of any communication is likely to be construed differently by various individuals it is at least a starting point to provide students with consistent information.

8 Problematizing assessment

Since students' talk about fairness in assessment is partly for sense-making purposes, we suggest that teachers actually instigate in-class discussions about assessment issues with their students. These class discussions would be in addition to establishing expectations and explaining course booklets. By promoting and encouraging discussion in class, students will realize that opinions and perceptions vary among their peers, and teachers will also be better informed about the diversity of student opinion. Stefani (1998) calls for a re-introduction of dialogue into the classroom, even when there are large numbers, and we suggest that much of this dialogue can be assessment-related. Teachers could raise an assessment issue or dilemma each week for brief discussion. For example, what should a teacher do if a student misses the submission time for an assignment by five minutes? If a student exceeds the 2,500 word count by 500 words, and their assignment is outstanding, should they be penalized? Pose the question: if a friend showed you their assignment and asked your opinion on whether it was unfairly marked, how honest do you think you would be? Teachers could use some of the vignettes presented in Chapter 2 of this book as starting points for conversation about assessment.

Returning students' work at least 15 minutes before the end of class, and remaining in the room, would give students the opportunity to engage in discussion with their teachers if they wish. In cases where work is submitted and returned electronically, an allocation of time in the next class for discussion would be necessary. With the students' permission, unidentifiable examples of assignments could be distributed for students to compare. This overt promotion of discussion and comparison would increase students' appreciation of the complexity of the assessment process, and demystify aspects of it.

Since effort is the main referent students use to gauge what they expect their grade to be, it would be useful for teachers to challenge their students' understanding about the role of effort and what effort entails (Adams 2005; Nesbit and Burton 2006). By engaging students in conversation about effort, students might become more discerning in their use of effort as a measure of input by which to judge the fairness of a grade. At the very least, they might begin to understand what amount of effort is required to achieve various results.

Teachers could highlight the dilemmas they face when they are expected to take into account personal circumstances, particularly when being approached for an extension on an assessment item. Teachers could declare to students that there is an element of trust involved, and that students are ultimately deceiving themselves if they make false claims.

9 Awarding grades and providing feedback

Tata refers to grades as the 'basic currency of our educational system' (1999: 263), which infers a medium of exchange in which students contribute their work, and the university assesses their work and awards them a grade. As a result, grades are important. They can have immediate and long-term consequences for students in terms of motivation for future study and work opportunities (Tata 1999). Students take their grades into account when they are considering the fairness of assessment. However, grades are not the sole indicator of students' perceptions of fairness.

It may well be true, as some suggest (MacDonald 1991; Winter *et al.* 1996; Rau and Durand 2000), that students pay particular attention to grades even though grades are usually accompanied by written or verbal feedback, but the feedback is still significant to students when making a fairness judgment.

Teachers could consider educating students about the time available to them for assessing student work, perhaps by explaining the nature of their academic workloads. Teachers might give students a choice about how they want their marking time allocated. For example, some students may prefer a mark with little feedback on one assignment, to enable more extensive and intensive feedback on another. Giving feedback to students without grades or marks is more likely to result in students reading the feedback. Black and Wiliam (1998) found this to have a significant positive impact on learning outcomes. One option is to present students with feedback followed at a later time by the grade. This gives them the opportunity to process the feedback without being distracted by the grade.

How feedback is expressed is equally as important as what is expressed (Falchikov and Boud 2007). Language used to provide feedback should be descriptive to ensure that there is a clear distinction between giving feedback on the product and on the person (Boud 1995). This might encourage previously shy or reluctant students to approach teachers to seek extra clarification about their assessment task. It is important that students discuss feedback that they do not understand. Teachers should ensure that students who are awarded outstanding grades also receive specific feedback that states which aspects of their work were particularly commendable and which aspects, even if minor, could be improved.

Many useful texts exist on providing feedback (for example: Falchikov 1995; Knight 1995; Race and Brown 1998; Race *et al.* 2005; Bryan and Clegg 2006). In recognizing that the sustainability of feedback is under threat in an era of mass higher education, Hounsell (2007) suggests there should be a greater focus on providing 'high-value' feedback. For example, teachers could involve students more in discussions about their work, and provide specific advice on how to improve future assessment items.

While Rust calls for departments to provide 'explicit guidelines on giving effective feedback' (2002: 156), Mutch (2003) suggests that this needs to be at the level of course and programme design as well as at the level of individual practice. Biggs and Tang (2007) recommend the 'constructive alignment' of assessment strategies, teaching methodologies and learning outcomes. To support this focus on providing effective feedback, it is imperative that more research is conducted that considers the student perspective (Weaver 2006).

10 Showing you care

The theory of demonstrating capability has shown that relationships are critical – that teaching and learning are relational and a caring relationship is more conducive to perceptions of fairness than a non-caring relationship. Teachers need to show that they care about students. It would be useful for students to realize that teachers show that they care in different ways. For some it might be that they have a passion for their subject matter; for others it is engaging in social pleasantries. As Noddings says, 'Taking a care perspective means we must consider the response of the cared-for' (1999: 13). Rather than arriving on time to teach a class, teachers could arrive a few minutes early and make conversation with students. They could say hello in passing and perhaps even comment on the message emblazoned across a t-shirt! This may seem superficial, but we have found that it is very important to students that they be acknowledged at a personal level. Teachers should ensure that they engage with all of their students, not only the keen, confident and/or mature age students. We found that students who perceive their teachers as caring about their well-being extend themselves to meet higher expectations. They accept more responsibility for their learning.

Representing students' perceptions of caring teachers as a continuum helps us to be aware of the range of teachers that students encounter in university life. As shown in Figure 6.1, at one end of the continuum there are teachers who are perceived by students as totally uncaring and, at the other, those who are genuinely caring. Where on this continuum do you think your students would place you?

As mentioned previously, students who perceive their teachers as caring accept more responsibility for their learning. There are many reasons why it is important that teachers care about their students. At the most fundamental level, it is part of the role of a teacher, it is a hallmark of good teaching and it makes a difference to students (Rogers and Webb 1991).

However, we acknowledge that other motivations to show you care might be influential. For example, student evaluations of teaching (SETs) are used in tertiary institutions to make judgments about continued employment, promotion, reputation of the staff member, and as a measure of student satisfaction, if not teaching effectiveness. Researchers argue the merits of SETs for measuring teaching effectiveness and learning, with some authors (Abrami *et al.* 1990; Marsh and Roche 1997, 2000) claiming they are useful in measuring teaching, and others (Marks 2000) questioning the validity of SETs for quantifying teaching effectiveness.

Regardless of the arguments, SETs cannot be ignored. Student satisfaction with a course is higher when students perceive their teachers as caring. As Teven and McCroskey (1996) report, students evaluate three aspects more positively if they perceive that person as caring: course content, amount of learning and the teacher themselves. Clayson and Sheffet (2006) found a strong connection between the personality of an instructor and a positive evaluation of that individual's teaching.

As Prosser and Trigwell state: 'We, as teachers, need to develop a sense of wonder about the variation in our students and our students' learning. We need to help our students develop a sense of wonder about our subject matter' (1999: 175). This is more likely to happen if there is a connection, or at least mutual respect, between teachers and students.

11 Supporting students to take action

Teachers want students to be autonomous learners, self-motivated and willing to accept responsibility for their learning. For this to happen, students need to develop the capacity for self-assessment and self-evaluation (Stefani 1998).

Figure 6.1 Continuum of students' perceptions of caring teachers

This means that they need to understand the criteria and the standards expected of them – and to take action if they do not. Teachers therefore need to be prepared to assist students to take action.

A student adopting a surviving response (such as not attending classes, going with the flow, or accepting failure and repeating) is at risk of opting out if their strategy does not work. These students are not easily identified because they generally do not interact with their teachers. The challenge for teachers is to encourage students to take action if they think they have been treated unfairly, rather than adopting a surviving response.

We recommend that teachers adopt a professional, detached approach when dealing with students who question a mark, seek a change of grade, seek further feedback or clarification about an assessment item, or lodge an appeal or official complaint. Clearly the way teachers respond to students' queries about assessment sets a precedent that either encourages students to take action to address their concerns, or to suppress them. Teachers have an important role in empowering students to take more responsibility for their learning, including taking action to address any problems with the assessment of their work. This is particularly important in increasing the likelihood of less confident students approaching teachers about assessment.

12 Being available for students

While appearing approachable is important, teachers also need to be physically accessible to students – that is, they need to tell students when they are available for consultation.

In their report on the first-year experience of students in Australian universities, Krause *et al.* (2005) show that there are many positive trends in relation to student perceptions of teaching when comparing results from 1994 and 2004 cohorts. But despite a positive shift in student perceptions of staff availability, they call for 'ongoing efforts to address the needs of those who continue to see teaching staff as "unavailable" or inaccessible' (2005: 83).

Teachers not only need to provide consultation hours, they need to encourage less confident students to use the time. To help students approach teaching staff, teachers need to consider whether they are making themselves available in an equitable way. It might seem obvious, but there is little point in teachers establishing consultation hours for internal students on a day when the students are not timetabled to be on campus.

Programme teams

1   Using the theory
2   Intervening early
3   Explaining options

1 Using the theory

The theory of demonstrating capability could be applied within each programme team, involving course coordinators and other teachers. Ideally a programme team would learn the process of demonstrating capability and ascertain which areas they need to address as a team, at course coordinator level, and at lecturer/tutor level. Involving students from a range of achievement levels – particularly low achievers – would be imperative. The involvement of students would assist the programme team in prioritizing areas of greatest need. Student involvement is also essential, as the theory challenges simplistic explanations of the fairness of assessment.

2 Intervening early

There is a need for early intervention schemes, early warning schemes or academic-alert systems so that teachers have a structured course of action in place to assist students in need or at risk. Such schemes would increase awareness of student needs and promote constructive, cooperative discussion among teachers. Hopefully the outcome would be fewer students opting out and withdrawing from university. These schemes would be the remit of programme teams.

One option for identifying the students who may be at risk is for programme teams to keep a running record of those who apply for extensions. The information gleaned from this could potentially support a student, as it might be an indicator of issues other than just a deficiency in time-management skills. Students could be referred to the university counselling service to assist in addressing their issues, or to a staff member in the programme who has the responsibility to follow up with identified students at risk.

Another group of students who may be identified as being at risk are those who fail a course and re-enrol. When students repeat a course, we recommend that teachers jointly work out a strategy with the student to reduce the chance of a repeat failure. In addition to helping them develop a plan of action, instigating a meeting might make the student feel that someone cares about them, and this alone might make the necessary difference to their effort. Programme teams need to coordinate this effort, as teachers may not realize that a student is repeating.

3 Explaining options

Students cannot take action if they do not know what options are available to them. Students need to learn which action is necessary for which problem, and when that action is most appropriate. Establishing mentor programmes across year levels that enable senior, experienced students to assist the new students is one option. This is particularly useful for students who may be reluctant to approach teachers.

There is a general realization by many in universities that a strategic approach to orientation programmes is necessary, with students being presented with information in a timely manner, and not being overwhelmed when they first arrive. This is the same with information about assessment processes – it would be timely for students to be reminded of the options they have at the point of having each assessment item returned, at least during first year. Programme teams could ensure that this is done across their courses.

Universities

One of the strengths of our approach was to elicit the personal experiences of students about assessment. Our approach tended to privilege personal experience over wider analyses of the policies and practices of the university. Our participants only rarely reflected on broader issues about assessment. This presented us with a challenge to go beyond these 'personal troubles' (Mills 1970: 9) to include university-wide practices that might be the fundamental source of students' difficulties. So, unfairness was viewed at a local level, usually at the level of the courses and the teachers, and occasionally at programme level. While students see the local context as being of primary importance, changes at an institutional level need to be made:

1   Problematizing assessment
2   Valuing teaching
3   Promoting access to teachers
4   Prioritizing first-year students.

1 Problematizing assessment

Universities could initiate campus-wide discussions about assessment among teachers and students. One of the aims of these discussions would be to assist students in developing a more sophisticated understanding of assessment. This would support the consultations within particular courses that are initiated by individual programme teams and teachers. An example of an assessment issue that could be discussed quite broadly is blind marking (assessment items submitted without the student's name). Another issue could be the responsibility universities have to provide explicit information about when students can apply for re-marking of an assessment item.

2 Valuing teaching

As much as students need care and attention in a university, so do the teachers. They are working in a system that is increasingly stretched for funds, their class sizes are increasing, and the time they have to allocate to teaching is diminishing as other responsibilities increase (including being an active researcher). Faced with their own survival needs, it is easy for teachers to forget the emotional impact assessment has on students. Teaching needs to be valued through the policies and practices of the university. Just as there are rewards for research achievements, there need to be substantial and valued rewards for teaching achievements.

Many teachers feel threatened by the increased level of evaluation by students, which they often view as being imposed on them. Our study shows that a few should feel threatened, as some current teaching practices are unacceptable. However, there are many exemplary teachers in universities who are under-utilized as role models for other teachers. Another problem is that some of the best teachers become administrators, in charge of coordinating sessional teaching staff and overseeing large classes. As a consequence, some of the best teachers reduce their face-to-face teaching role with students.

Teachers who are keen to improve their teaching could form professional development teams and utilize the skills of the recipients of university teaching awards. Perhaps the recipients of awards would be prepared to have small groups of teachers observe their teaching and critique it afterwards. To further assist teachers – most importantly, the course coordinators – we recommend that staff well-versed in assessment be available to advise them about refining, modifying and changing their assessment practices.

3 Promoting access to teachers

Our study has shown that student access to teachers is important. This is not new knowledge. In 1985 Astin said that:

> A large body of research suggests that the best way to involve students in learning and college life is to maximize the amount of personal contact between faculty members and students. Unfortunately, the policies of many institutions militate against such contact.
>
> (1985: 162)

For students to have access to teachers there are implications for staff development, flexible work arrangements and the employment policies of the universities. When involved in teaching, teachers need to be available to students – to honour their 'office hours' and have the 'head space' for students.

There is obviously an issue of finding a workload balance that allows teachers to provide the educational experience students require while coping with the other demands of an academic life. This balance needs to be found so that teachers have the 'personal well-being that comes from not feeling overwhelmed and overworked [which] allows us to bring enthusiasm and a positive attitude to our role as educator' (Smart *et al.* 1999: 214). One option to address this issue is to have academic staff alternate between teaching and research commitments rather than run them concurrently. Another option is to allow staff to overload in one semester and have a lesser teaching load in the following semester.

4 Prioritizing first-year students

Finally, skilful teachers need to work with first-year students. These are the most vulnerable students; they are the least likely to question assessment practices and the ones who would benefit the most if they did. Most students are not goal-orientated and self-directed learners at the point of beginning university; if skilful teachers taught first-year students, the students would become autonomous learners more quickly. This would reduce the issues that develop in later years when the stakes get higher.

Further research

Further grounded theory research could be conducted to broaden the applicability of the theory of demonstrating capability, by exploring perceptions of fairness of assessment with external students, international students and students from broad fields of study not represented in this research. In doing this, the content of each stage could be further refined. The modifiability of this grounded theory allows for this.

The demonstrating capability theory also provides scope for future quantitative research. Another area for future research is to track individual students' experiences of assessment across their university programme. The aim of this would be to identify specific strategies that would increase the likelihood of students responding to perceptions of unfairness in assessment by taking action, rather than opting out. Likewise, future research could examine what helps to move students from adopting a surviving response to a taking action response.

This theory provides possibilities for future research aimed at refining the content of student evaluations of teaching and course experience questionnaires. Following this, courses in which satisfaction with assessment is high could be examined to develop further our understanding of what contributes to high levels of satisfaction. This would involve analysing course booklets, observing teaching and perhaps observing the interaction between teachers and students during 'office' hours.

We mentioned earlier in the book that students' perceptions of the fairness of assessment are strongly linked to the quality of feedback that they receive from their teachers. Given the importance of feedback it follows that more research should be conducted in this area.

Finally, a parallel study could be conducted looking at the perspective of teachers – how they perceive and construct fairness of assessment within the context of their pedagogical philosophy and intentions.

Conclusion

Given that students' perceptions of the fairness of assessment are nuanced, individualized and complex, it is a pleasure for us to be able to present to the academic world a theory that explains what students take into account when they decide whether assessment is fair, what they do if it is unfair, and what influences their response to unfair assessment. This is the theory of demonstrating capability.

We have heard teachers say that students think that assessment is fair if they pass their assignments, and that they like teachers who are not tough markers. We heard an academic staff member inducting new teachers into the university saying: 'Assessment is fair to students if it is relevant, full stop. Don't worry about anything else; just make sure it is relevant.' These simplistic and naïve understandings of students' views trivialize what is an extremely important issue for students: assessment. Assessment surrounds all that they do at university; it drives their learning and their behaviour. By understanding what students really mean by fairness in assessment, by improving our assessment practices and our communication with students, we can improve our teaching and improve the university experience for our students.

Glossary

Assessment policy and procedure manual Manual that describes the policies and procedural matters related to assessment in a university.

CEI (course evaluation instrument) Course evaluation instrument questionnaire, conducted anonymously, to collect systematic student feedback about the students' experience of a course.

Conceded pass A pass that permits a student to use the course as a prerequisite for another course. Conceded passes are in the range of 45–49 per cent, which is usually regarded as a fail. They are awarded by a committee as part of a review of student progress and are based on consideration of the student's overall results. There is a maximum number that can be awarded in a programme.

Core course A course that is compulsory for the student to study in a programme.

Course An individual subject within a programme (degree), e.g. Mathematics 101.

Course booklets Booklets or course outlines given to students at the beginning of a course that outline the aims and requirements of the course being studied.

Course coordinator The staff member responsible for a course.

Demonstrating capability This is the process students engage in to address their experience of frustration with assessment. It has two stages: deciding the fairness of assessment, and responding to unfair assessment.

Elective course A course that is optional for a student to study. Many programmes specify a minimum and maximum number of elective courses a student must complete.

Feedback-seeking cycle This describes the four implications for students who seek feedback. (1) Perceptions of control increase and stress decreases. (2) Receiving feedback allows the student to transform a more complex task into a simpler task, further decreasing stress. (3) Receiving feedback and making necessary changes might mean mistakes or bad habits or misunderstandings might not be repeated. (4) Gives students a better appreciation of how they can take control of their own learning, and of how they are responsible for their own learning.

Grading system   When grades are referred to in this book they are from a system where grades awarded can be high distinction (HD, 85–100%), distinction (D, 75–84%), credit (C, 65–74%), pass level 1 (P1, 55–64%), pass level 2 (P2, 50–54%), fail level 1 (F1, 40–49%), fail level 2 (F2, below 40%).

Head of school   The staff member responsible for a school within the university, e.g. Head of School of Education, Head of School of Computer and Information Science.

Honours degree   A separate, stand-alone one-year programme of advanced studies for students who demonstrate a high level of achievement on completion of their pass degree programme.

Opting out   One of the responses students have to unfair assessment. Opting out refers to the behaviour of students who decide not to continue in a course, programme or the university because they feel that they have no choice but to withdraw.

Programme   A university degree, e.g. Bachelor of Arts.

Programme director   The staff member responsible for a programme within a school. Within the programme there will be a number of courses.

Response modifiers   These describe the conditions that influence the actions students take if they perceive assessment to be unfair.

SET (student evaluation of teaching)   Student evaluation of teaching questionnaire, conducted anonymously, towards the end of a teaching period to collect systematic student feedback on teaching for the purpose of improving teaching practice, or applying for promotion.

Surviving   A surviving response is a relatively passive response to dealing with a perception of unfair assessment. It enables a student to endure a situation in the short term but does not necessarily advance them from the position they are in.

TAFE (Technical and Further Education)   Technical and Further Education is the largest vocational education and training provider in Australia.

Taking action   The most proactive of the student responses to a perception of unfair assessment. It includes action such as seeking feedback or explanations, seeking a change of grade or re-mark, or lodging an official appeal/complaint.

Teachers   In this book, 'teachers' refers to staff who have a teaching role, e.g. academic staff, lecturers, tutors and assessors.

Terminating pass   A pass that does not permit a student to use the course as a prerequisite for another course. Terminating passes are in the range of 45–49 per cent, which is usually regarded as a fail. They are awarded by a committee as part of a review of student progress and are based on consideration of the student's overall results. There is a maximum number that can be awarded in a programme.

Bibliography

Abrami, PC, D'Appollonia, S and Cohen, PA (1990) 'Validity of student ratings of instruction: what we know and what we do not', *Journal of Educational Psychology*, vol. 82, no. 2, pp. 219–31.

Adams, JB (2005) 'What makes the grade? Faculty and student perceptions', *Teaching and Psychology*, vol. 32, no. 1, pp. 21–5.

Adams, JS (1963) 'Toward an understanding of inequity', *Journal of Abnormal and Social Psychology*, vol. 67, pp. 422–36.

Adams, JS (1965) 'Inequity in social exchange', *Advances in Experimental Social Psychology*, vol. 2, pp. 267–99.

Anderman, EM, Noar, SM, Zimmerman, RS and Donohew, L (2004) 'The need for sensation as a prerequisite for motivation to engage in academic tasks', in *Motivating students, improving schools: the legacy of Carol Midgley*, vol. 13, eds PR Pintrich and ML Maehr, Elsevier, Amsterdam, pp. 1–26.

Anderson, LE and Carta-Falsa, J (2002) 'Factors that make faculty and student relationships effective', *College Teaching*, vol. 50, no. 4, pp. 134–8.

Argyris, C (1960) *Understanding organizational behavior*, Dorsey Press, Homewood, IL.

Ashworth, P, Bannister, P and Thorne, P (1997) 'Guilty in whose eyes? University students' perceptions of cheating and plagiarism in academic work and assessment', *Studies in Higher Education*, vol. 22, no. 2, pp. 187–203.

Assessment Standards Knowledge exchange (ASKe) (no date) ASKe website, Centre of Excellence for Teaching and Learning, Oxford Brookes University Business School, www.brookes.ac.uk/aske [accessed 30 August 2010].

Astin, AW (1985) *Achieving educational excellence: a critical assessment of priorities and practices in higher education*, Jossey-Bass, San Francisco, CA.

Augoustinos, M, Tuffin, K and Every, D (2005) 'New racism, meritocracy and individualism: constraining affirmative action in education', *Discourse & Society*, vol. 16, no. 3, pp. 315–40.

Australian National University (2008) 'Public opinion towards higher education: results from the ANU poll – Report 2', ANU, Canberra.

Ball, SJ (2003) 'The teacher's soul and the terrors of performativity', *Journal of Education Policy*, vol. 18, no. 2, pp. 215–28.

Ballantyne, R, Bain, J and Packer, J (eds) (1997) *Reflecting on university teaching: academics' stories*, Australian Government Publishing Service, Canberra.

Bandura, A (1977) 'Self-efficacy: toward a unifying theory of behavioral change', *Psychological Review*, vol. 84, pp. 191–215.

Bandura, A (1986) *Social foundations of thought and action: a social cognitive theory*, Prentice-Hall, Englewood Cliffs, NJ.

Bandura, A (1993) 'Perceived self-efficacy in cognitive development and functioning', *Educational Psychologist*, vol. 28, no. 2, pp. 117–48.

Barfield, RL (2003) 'Students' perceptions of and satisfaction with group grades and the group experience in the college classroom', *Assessment and Evaluation in Higher Education*, vol. 28, no. 4, pp. 355–69.

Barker, P (1998) *Michel Foucault: an introduction*, Edinburgh University Press, Edinburgh.

Bernstein, B (1971) 'On the classification and framing of educational knowledge', in *Knowledge and control: new directions for the sociology of education*, ed. MFD Young, Collier-Macmillan, London, pp. 47–69.

Bies, RJ and Moag, JF (1986) 'Interactional justice: communication criteria of fairness', in *Research on negotiations in organizations*, vol. 1, eds RJ Lewicki, BH Sheppard and MH Bazerman, JAI Press, Greenwich, CT, pp. 43–55.

Biggs, J (2003) *Teaching for quality learning at university: what the student does*, 2nd edn, Society for Research into Higher Education and Open University Press, Buckingham.

Biggs, J and Tang, C (2007) *Teaching for quality learning at university: what the student does*, 3rd edn, McGraw-Hill/Society for Research into Higher Education and Open University Press, Maidenhead.

Bjørnskov, C, Dreher, A, Fischer, J and Schnellenbach, J (2009) On the relation between income inequality and happiness: do fairness perceptions matter? KOF working papers 09–245, KOF Swiss Economic Institute, Zurich, http://ideas. repec.org/p/kof/wpskof/09–245.html [accessed 10 May 2010].

Black, P and Wiliam, D (1998) 'Assessment and classroom learning', *Assessment in Education: Principles, Policy and Practice*, vol. 5, no. 3, pp. 7–74.

Blowers, P (2006) 'Using student skill self-assessments to get balanced groups for group projects', *College Teaching*, vol. 51, no. 3, pp. 106–10.

Bloxham, S and West, A (2004) 'Understanding the rules of the game: marking peer assessment as a medium for developing students' conceptions of assessment', *Assessment and Evaluation in Higher Education*, vol. 29, no. 6, pp. 721–33.

Bogdan, R and Biklen, S (1992) *Qualitative research for education: an introduction to theory and methods*, 2nd edn, Allyn & Bacon, Boston, MA.

Boud, D (1995) 'Assessment and learning: contradictory or complementary', in *Assessment for learning in higher education*, ed. P Knight, Kogan Page, London, pp. 35–48.

Boud, D and Falchikov, N (eds) (2007) *Rethinking assessment in higher education: learning for the longer term*, Routledge, London.

Bowles, S and Gintis, H (1976) *Schooling in capitalist America: educational reform and contradictions of economic life*, Routledge & Kegan Paul, London.

Brown, G (1997) *Assessing student learning in higher education*, Routledge, London.

Brown, S and Glasner, A (eds) (1999) *Assessment matters in higher education: choosing and using diverse approaches*, Society for Research into Higher Education and Open University Press, Buckingham.

Brown, S and Knight, P (1994) *Assessing learners in higher education*, Kogan Page, London.

Bryan, C and Clegg, K (eds) (2006) *Innovative assessment in higher education*, Routledge, London and New York.

Burdett, J (2003) 'Making groups work: university students' perceptions', *International Education Journal*, vol. 4, no. 3, pp. 177–91.

Canaan, JE (1997) 'Examining the examination: tracing the effects of pedagogic authority on cultural studies lecturers and students', in *A question of discipline: pedagogy, power, and the teaching of cultural studies*, eds JE Canaan and D Epstein, Westview Press, Boulder, CO, pp. 157–77.

Canaan, J and Shumar, W (2008a) 'Higher education in the era of globalization and neoliberalism', in *Structure and agency in the neoliberal university*, eds J Canaan and W Shumar, Routledge, London, pp. 3–29.

Canaan, J and Shumar, W (eds) (2008b) *Structure and agency in the neoliberal university*, Routledge, London.

Carless, D, Joughin, G and Liu, N-F (2006) *How assessment supports learning: learning oriented assessment in action*, Hong Kong University Press, Hong Kong.

Chapman, KJ and Van Auken, S (2001) 'Creating positive group project experiences: an examination of the role of the instructor on students' perceptions of group projects', *Journal of Marketing Education*, vol. 23, no. 2, pp. 117–27.

Charmaz, K (2006) *Constructing grounded theory: a practical guide through qualitative analysis*, Sage, London.

Chenitz, WC (1986) 'Getting started: the research proposal for a grounded theory study', in *From practice to grounded theory: qualitative research in nursing*, eds WC Chenitz and JM Swanson, Addison-Wesley Publishing Company, Menlo Park, CA, pp. 39–47.

Clayson, DE and Haley, DA (1990) 'Student evaluations in marketing: what is actually being measured?' *Journal of Marketing Education*, vol. 12, pp. 9–17.

Clayson, DE and Sheffet, MJ (2006) 'Personality and the student evaluation of teaching', *Journal of Marketing Education*, vol. 28, no. 2, pp. 149–60.

Clegg, K and Bryan, C (2006) 'Reflections, rationales and realities', in *Innovative assessment in higher education*, eds C Bryan and K Clegg, Routledge, London, pp. 216–27.

Colquitt, JA (2001) 'On the dimensionality of organizational justice: a construct validation of a measure', *Journal of Applied Psychology*, vol. 86, no. 3, pp. 386–400.

Crooks, TJ (1988) 'The impact of classroom evaluation practices on students', *Review of Educational Research*, vol. 58, no. 4, pp. 438–81.

Crossman, J (2004) 'Factors influencing the assessment perceptions of training teachers', *International Education Journal*, vol. 5, no. 4, pp. 582–90.

Denk, CE, Benson, JM, Fletcher, JC and Reigel, TM (1997) 'How do Americans want to die? A factorial vignette survey of public attitudes about end-of-life medical decision-making', *Social Science Research*, vol. 26, pp. 95–120.

Divaharan, S and Atputhasamy, L (2002) 'An attempt to enhance the quality of cooperative learning through peer assessment', *Journal of Educational Enquiry*, vol. 3, no. 2, pp. 72–83.

Dochy, F, Segers, M and Sluijsmans, D (1999) 'The use of self-, peer and co-assessment in higher education: a review', *Studies in Higher Education*, vol. 24, no. 3, pp. 331–50.

Dowling, R (2008) 'Geographies of identity: labouring in the "neoliberal" university', *Progress in Human Geography*, vol. 32, no. 6, pp. 812–20.

Drew, S (2001) 'Student perceptions of what helps them learn and develop in higher education', *Teaching in Higher Education*, vol. 6, no. 3, pp. 309–31.

D'Souza, SM and Wood, LN (2003) 'Tertiary students' views about group work in mathematics', paper presented at the Australian Association for Research in Education Conference, Auckland, New Zealand, November.

Duffield, KE and Spencer, A (2002) 'A survey of medical students' views about the purposes and fairness of assessment', *Medical Education*, vol. 36, no. 9, pp. 879–86.

Dunn, L, Morgan, C, O'Reilly, M and Parry, S (2004) *The student assessment handbook: new directions in traditional and online assessment*, RoutledgeFalmer, London.

Dweck, CS (2007) 'The perils and promises of praise', *Educational Leadership*, vol. 65, no. 2, pp. 34–9.

Emanuel, R and Adams, JN (2006) 'Assessing college student perceptions of instructor customer service via the quality of instructor service to students (QISS) questionnaire', *Assessment and Evaluation in Higher Education*, vol. 31, no. 5, pp. 535–49.

Everton, WJ, Jolton, JA and Mastrangelo, PM (2007) 'Be nice and fair or else: understanding reasons for employees' deviant behaviors', *Journal of Management Development*, vol. 26, no. 2, pp. 117–31.

Falchikov, N (1995) 'Improving feedback to and from students', in *Assessment for learning in higher education*, ed. P Knight, RoutledgeFalmer, London, pp. 157–66.

Falchikov, N (2005) *Improving feedback through student involvement*, Routledge-Falmer, London.

Falchikov, N (2007) 'The place of peers in learning and assessment', in *Rethinking assessment in higher education: learning for the longer term*, eds D Boud and N Falchikov, Routledge, London, pp. 128–43.

Falchikov, N and Boud, D (2007) 'Assessment and emotion: the impact of being assessed', in *Rethinking assessment in higher education: learning for the longer term*, eds D Boud and N Falchikov, Routledge, London, pp. 144–55.

Farwell, L and Weiner, B (1996) 'Self-perceptions of fairness in individual and group contexts', *Personality and Social Psychology Bulletin*, vol. 22, no. 9, pp. 868–81.

Fitzgerald, RT (Commissioner) (1976) *Poverty and education in Australia: Commission of Inquiry into Poverty (Fifth main report)*, Australian Government Publishing Service, Canberra.

Flanagan, C, Campbell, B, Botcheva, L, Bowes, J, Csapo, B *et al.* (2003) 'Social class and adolescents' beliefs about justice in different social orders', *Journal of Social Issues*, vol. 59, no. 4, pp. 711–32.

Fleming, ND (1999) 'Biases in marking students' written work: quality?' in *Assessment matters in higher education: choosing and using diverse approaches*, eds S Brown and A Glasner, Society for Research into Higher Education and Open University Press, Buckingham, pp. 83–92.

Foucault, M (1977) *Discipline and punish: the birth of the prison*, Allen Lane, London.

Foucault, M (1980) *Power/knowledge: selected interviews and other writings 1972–1977*, Harvester Press, Sussex.

Freeman, M and McKenzie, J (2002) 'SPARK, a confidential web-based template for self and peer assessment of student teamwork: benefits of evaluating across different subjects', *British Journal of Educational Technology*, vol. 33, no. 5, pp. 551–69.

Frymier, AB and Houser, ML (2000) 'The teacher–student relationship as an interpersonal relationship', *Communication Education*, vol. 49, no. 3, pp. 207–19.

Gale, T, Sellar, S, Parker, S, Hattam, R, Comber, B *et al.* (2010) 'Interventions early in school as a means to improve higher education outcomes for disadvantaged (particularly low SES) students: a design and evaluation matrix for university outreach in schools', DEEWR, Canberra, www.deewr.gov.au/HigherEducation/Publications/Documents/Synopsis.rtf [accessed 12 February 2010].

Gatfield, T (1999) 'Examining student satisfaction with group projects and peer assessment', *Assessment and Evaluation in Higher Education*, vol. 2, no. 4, pp. 365–77.

Gibbs, G (1999) 'Using assessment strategically to change the way students learn', in *Assessment matters in higher education: choosing and using diverse approaches*, eds S Brown and A Glasner, Society for Research into Higher Education and Open University Press, Buckingham, pp. 41–53.

Gibbs, G (2006) 'Why assessment is changing', in *Innovative assessment in higher education*, eds C Bryan and K Clegg, Routledge, London, pp. 11–22.

Gillespie, K (2010) 'ANZAC Day address', reported in *The Weekend Australian*, 24–5 April 2010, pp. 8–9.

Gillespie, M (2005) 'Student–teacher connection: a place of possibility', *Journal of Advanced Nursing*, vol. 52, no. 2, pp. 211–19.

Gipps, CV (1994) *Beyond testing: towards a theory of educational assessment*, Falmer Press, London.

Glaser, BG (1978) *Theoretical sensitivity*, Sociology Press, Mill Valley, CA.

Glaser, BG (1992) *Basics of grounded theory analysis: emergence vs forcing*, Sociology Press, Mill Valley, CA.

Glaser, BG (1998) *Doing grounded theory: issues and discussions*, Sociology Press, Mill Valley, CA.

Glaser, BG (2001) *The grounded theory perspective: conceptualization contrasted with description*, Sociology Press, Mill Valley, CA.

Glaser, BG and Strauss, AL (1967) *The discovery of grounded theory: strategies for qualitative research*, Aldine de Gruyter, New York.

Goleman, D (1985) *Vital lies, simple truths: the psychology of self-deception*, Simon & Schuster, New York.

Gore, JM (1995) 'On the continuity of power relations in pedagogy', *International Studies in Sociology of Education*, vol. 5, no. 2, pp. 165–88.

Gorham, J and Christophel, DM (1992) 'Students' perceptions of teacher behaviors as motivating and demotivating factors in college classes', *Communication Quarterly*, vol. 40, pp. 239–52.

Gorham, J and Millette, DM (1997) 'A comparative analysis of teacher and student perceptions of sources of motivation and demotivation in college classes', *Communication Education*, vol. 46, pp. 245–61.

Greenberg, J (2005) *Managing behavior in organizations*, 4th edn, Pearson Prentice Hall, Upper Saddle River, NJ.

Gupta, ML (2004) 'Enhancing student performance through cooperative learning in physical sciences', *Assessment and Evaluation in Higher Education*, vol. 29, no. 1, pp. 63–73.

Hadzigeorgiou, Y (2001) 'Some thoughts on the notion of purposeful learning', *The Educational Forum*, vol. 64, no. 4, pp. 316–25.

Henry, N (2009) *A fair Australia*, The Australian Collaboration, www. australiancollaboration.com.au/_factsheets/1.%20FairAustralia_FactSheet.pdf [accessed 12 May 2010].

Higgins, R, Hartley, P and Skelton, A (2002) 'The conscientious consumer: reconsidering the role of assessment feedback in student learning', *Studies in Higher Education*, vol. 27, no. 1, p. 2002.

Holstein, JA and Gubrium, JF (1995) *The active interview*, Sage, Thousand Oaks, CA.

Hounsell, D (2007) 'Towards more sustainable feedback', in *Rethinking assessment in higher education: learning for the longer term*, eds D Boud and N Falchikov, Routledge, London, pp. 101–13.

Houston, MB and Bettencourt, LA (1999) 'But that's not fair! An exploratory study of student perceptions of instructor fairness', *Journal of Marketing Education*, vol. 21, no. 2, pp. 84–96.

John, CS and Bates, NA (1990) 'Racial composition and neighbourhood evaluation', *Social Science Research*, vol. 19, no. 1, pp. 47–61.

Johnson, B (2000) 'Using video vignettes to evaluate children's personal safety knowledge: methodological and ethical issues', *Child Abuse and Neglect: The International Journal*, vol. 24, no. 6, pp. 811–27.

Jones, R and Noble, G (2007) 'Grounded theory and management research: a lack of integrity?' *Qualitative Research in Organisations and Management: An International Journal*, vol. 2, no. 2, pp. 84–103.

Kaplan, A (2000) 'Teacher and student: designing a democratic relationship', *Journal of Curriculum Studies*, vol. 32, no. 3, pp. 377–402.

Karau, SJ and Williams, KD (1993) 'Social loafing: a meta-analytic review and theoretical integration', *Journal of Personality and Social Psychology*, vol. 65, no. 4, pp. 681–706.

Kennedy, GJ (2005) 'Peer-assessment in group projects: is it worth it?' paper presented at the Seventh Australasian Computing Education Conference, Newcastle, Australia, January/February.

Killen, R (1994) 'Differences between students' and lecturers' perceptions of factors influencing students' academic success at university', *Higher Education Research and Development*, vol. 13, no. 2, pp. 199–211.

Knight, P (ed.) (1995) *Assessment for learning in higher education*, RoutledgeFalmer, Abingdon.

Kniveton, BH (1996) 'Student perceptions of assessment methods', *Assessment and Evaluation in Higher Education*, vol. 21, no. 3, pp. 229–37.

Krause, K-L, Hartley, R, James, R and McInnis, C (2005) *The first year experience in Australian universities: findings from a decade of national studies*, Department of Education, Science and Training, Canberra.

Leach, L, Neutze, G and Zepke, N (2001) 'Assessment and empowerment: some critical questions', *Assessment and Evaluation in Higher Education*, vol. 26, no. 4, pp. 293–305.

Lejk, M, Wyvill, M and Farrow, S (1996) 'A survey of methods of deriving individual grades from group assessments', *Assessment and Evaluation in Higher Education*, vol. 21, no. 3, pp. 267–80.

Leventhal, GS (1980) 'What should be done with equity theory? New approaches to the study of fairness in social relationships', in *Social exchange: advances in theory and research*, eds KJ Gergen, MS Greenberg and RH Willis, Plenum Press, New York, pp. 27–55.

Leventhal, GS, Karusa, J and Fry, WR (1980) 'Beyond fairness: a theory of allocation preferences', in *Justice and social interaction*, ed. G Mikula, Springer-Verlag, New York, pp. 167–218.

Levinson, H, Price, C, Munden, K and Solley, C (1962) *Men, management and mental health*, Harvard University Press, Cambridge, MA.

Lyotard, J (1984 [1979]) *The post-modern condition: a report on knowledge*, trans. G Bennington and B Massumi, Manchester University Press, Manchester.

McCoubrie, P (2004) 'Improving the fairness of multiple-choice questions: a literature review', *Medical Teacher*, vol. 26, no. 8, pp. 709–12.

MacDonald, RB (1991) 'Developmental students' processing of teacher feedback in composition instruction', *Review of Research in Developmental Education*, vol. 8, no. 5, pp. 3–7.

McDowell, L and Sambell, K (1999) 'The experience of innovative assessment: student perspectives', in *Assessment matters in higher education: choosing and using diverse approaches*, eds S Brown and A Glasner, Society for Research into Higher Education and Open University Press, Buckingham, pp. 71–82.

McHoul, A and Grace, W (1993) *A Foucault primer: discourse, power and the subject*, Melbourne University Press, Melbourne.

McInnis, C and Hartley, R (2002) *Managing study and work: the impact of full-time study and paid work on the undergraduate experiences in Australian universities*, Evaluations and Investigations Programme, Commonwealth Department of Education, Science and Training, Canberra.

McKeganey, N, Abel, M and Hay, G (1996) 'Contrasting methods of collecting data on injectors' risk behaviour', *AIDS Care*, vol. 8, no. 5, pp. 557–63.

Maehr, M and Pintrich, PR (eds) (1991) *Advances in motivation and achievement: goals and self-regulatory processes*, JAI Press, Greenwich.

Marks, RB (2000) 'Determinants of student evaluations of global measures of instructor and course value', *Journal of Marketing Education*, vol. 22, no. 2, pp. 108–19.

Marsh, HW and Roche, LA (1997) 'Making students' evaluations of teaching effectiveness effective: the critical issues of validity, bias, and utility', *American Psychologist*, vol. 52, no. 11, pp. 1187–97.

Marsh, HW and Roche, LA (2000) 'Effects of grading leniency and low workload on students' evaluations of teaching: popular myth, bias, validity, or innocent bystanders?' *Journal of Educational Psychology*, vol. 92, no. 1, pp. 202–28.

Marsh, HW, Walker, R and Debus, R (1991) 'Subject-specific components of academic self-concept and self-efficacy', *Contemporary Educational Psychology*, vol. 16, no. 4, pp. 331–45.

Marshall, G, Swift, A, Routh, D and Burgoyne, C (1999) 'What is and what ought to be?: Popular beliefs about distributive justice in thirteen countries', *European Sociological Review*, vol. 15, no. 4, pp. 349–67.

Marshall, JD (1996) *Michel Foucault: personal autonomy and education*, Kluwer Academic Publishers, Dordrecht.

Massingham, P and Herrington, T (2006) 'Does attendance matter? An examination of students' attitudes, participation, performance, and attendance', *Journal of University Teaching and Learning Practice*, vol. 3, no. 2, pp. 82–103.

Mateju, P (1997) 'Beliefs about distributive justice and social change', working paper 6/1997 of the research project 'Social Trends', http://archiv.soc.cas.cz/download/66/97–6.doc [accessed 10 May 2010].

Michaels, JW and Miethe, TD (1989) 'Academic effort and college grades', *Social Forces*, vol. 68, no. 1, pp. 309–19.

Millar, D (1992) 'Distributive justice: what the people think', *Ethics*, vol. 102, pp. 555–93.

Miller, AH, Imrie, BW and Cox, K (1998) *Student assessment in higher education: a handbook for assessing performance*, Kogan Page, London.

Miller, JL, Rossi, PH and Simpson, JE (1986) 'Perceptions of justice: race and gender differences in judgments of appropriate prison sentences', *Law and Society Review*, vol. 20, no. 3, pp. 312–34.

Mills, CW (1970) *The sociological imagination*, Penguin, Harmondsworth.

Mills, P (2003) 'Group project work with undergraduate veterinary science students', *Assessment and Evaluation in Higher Education*, vol. 28, no. 5, pp. 527–38.

Minichiello, V, Aroni, R, Timewell, E and Alexander, L (1995) *In-depth interviewing: principles, techniques, analysis*, 2nd edn, Longman Cheshire, Melbourne.

Mutch, A (2003) 'Exploring the practice of feedback to students', *Active Learning in Higher Education*, vol. 4, no. 1, pp. 24–38.

Nelson-Le Gall, S and Scott-Jones, D (1985) 'Teachers' and young children's perceptions of appropriate work strategies', *Child Study Journal*, vol. 15, no. 1, pp. 29–42.

Nesbit, PL and Burton, S (2006) 'Student justice perceptions following assignment feedback', *Assessment and Evaluation in Higher Education*, vol. 31, no. 6, pp. 655–70.

Noddings, N (1999) 'Care, justice and equity', in *Justice and caring: the search for common ground in education*, eds MS Katz, N Noddings and KA Strike, Teachers College Press, New York, pp. 7–20.

Pajares, F (1996) 'Self-efficacy beliefs in academic settings', *Review of Educational Research*, vol. 66, no. 4, pp. 543–78.

Pickett, K and Wilkinson, R (2010) *The spirit level: why greater equality makes society stronger*, Bloomsbury Press, New York.

Pintrich, PR and Schunk, DH (1995) *Motivation in education: theory, research, and applications*, Prentice Hall, Englewood Cliffs, NJ.

Pintrich, PR and Maehr, ML (eds) (2004) *Motivating students, improving schools: the legacy of Carol Midgley*, Elsevier, Amsterdam.

Pojman, L (2001) 'Justice as desert', *Queensland University of Technology Law and Justice Journal*, vol. 7, www.austlii.edu.au/au/journals/QUTLJJ/2001/7.html [accessed 12 February 2010].

Price, M (2005) 'Assessment standards: the role of communities of practice and the scholarship of assessment', *Assessment and Evaluation in Higher Education*, vol. 30, no. 3, pp. 215–30.

Prosser, M and Trigwell, K (1999) *Understanding learning and teaching: the experience in higher education*, Society for Research into Higher Education and Open University Press, Buckingham.

Rabinow, P (ed.) (1984) *The Foucault reader*, Penguin, London.

Race, P (1995) 'What has assessment done for us – and to us?' in *Assessment for learning in higher education*, ed. P Knight, RoutledgeFalmer, Abingdon, pp. 61–74.

Race, P and Brown, S (1998) *The lecturer's toolkit: a practical guide to teaching, learning and assessment*, Kogan Page, London.

Race, P, Brown, S and Smith, B (2005) *500 tips on assessment*, 2nd edn, Routledge Falmer, London.

Rahman, N (1996) 'Caregivers' sensitivity to conflict: the use of the vignette methodology', *Journal of Elder Abuse and Neglect*, vol. 8, no. 1, pp. 35–47.

Ramsden, P (2003) *Learning to teach in higher education*, 2nd edn, RoutledgeFalmer, London.

Rau, W and Durand, A (2000) 'The academic ethic and college grades: does hard work help students to "make the grade"?' *Sociology of Education*, vol. 73, pp. 19–38.

Rawls, J (1971) *A theory of justice*, Oxford University Press, London.

Robertson, J (2006) ' "If you know our names it helps!" Students' perspectives about "good" teaching', *Qualitative Inquiry*, vol. 12, no. 4, pp. 756–68.

Robinson, CF and Kakela, PJ (2006) 'Creating a space to learn: a classroom of fun, interaction, and trust', *College Teaching*, vol. 54, no. 1, pp. 202–6.

Rogers, D and Webb, J (1991) 'The ethic of caring in teacher education', *Journal of Teacher Education*, vol. 42, no. 3, pp. 172–81.

Roper, T (1970) *The myth of equality*, Australian Union of Students, Melbourne.

Rowntree, D (1987) *Assessing students: how shall we know them?*, revised edn, Kogan Page, London.

Rust, C (2002) 'The impact of assessment on student learning: how can the research literature practically help to inform the development of departmental assessment strategies and learner-centred assessment practices?', *Active Learning in Higher Education*, vol. 3, no. 2, pp. 145–58.

Rust, C, Price, M and O'Donovan, B (2003) 'Improving students' learning by developing their understanding of assessment criteria and processes', *Assessment and Evaluation in Higher Education*, vol. 28, no. 2, pp. 147–64.

Sambell, K and McDowell, L (1997) 'The value of self and peer assessment to the developing lifelong learner', in *Improving student learning: improving students as learners*, ed. C Rust, Oxford Centre for Staff and Learning Development, Oxford, pp. 56–66.

Sambell, K, McDowell, L and Brown, S (1997) ' "But is it fair?": An exploratory study of student perceptions of the consequential validity of assessment', *Studies in Educational Evaluation*, vol. 23, no. 4, pp. 349–71.

Schein, E (1965) *Organizational psychology*, Prentice Hall, Englewood Cliffs, NJ.

Schein, E (1992) *Organizational culture and leadership*, 2nd edn, Jossey-Bass, San Francisco, CA.

Schön, DA (1983) *The reflective practitioner*, Basic Books, New York.

Schön, DA (1987) *Educating the reflective practitioner*, Jossey-Bass, San Francisco, CA.

Schön, DA (1991) *The reflective turn: case studies in and on educational practice*, Teachers Press, New York.

Schuman, H, Walsh, E, Olson, C and Etheridge, B (1985) 'Effort and reward: the assumption that college grades are affected by quantity of study', *Social Forces*, vol. 63, no. 4, pp. 945–66.

Schunk, DH (1990) 'Goal setting and self-efficacy during self-regulated learning', *Educational Psychologist*, vol. 25, no. 1, pp. 71–86.

Schunk, DH (1991) 'Self-efficacy and academic motivation', *Educational Psychologist*, vol. 26, no. 3, pp. 207–31.

Scott, G (2006) *Accessing the student voice: using CEQuery to identify what retains students and promotes engagement in productive learning in Australian higher education*, Department of Education, Science and Training, Canberra.

Sias, PM and Jablin, FM (1995) 'Differential superior–subordinate relations, perceptions of fairness, and coworker communication', *Human Communication Research*, vol. 22, no. 1, pp. 5–38.

Smart, DT, Kelley, CA and Conant, JS (1999) 'Marketing education in the year 2000: changes observed and challenges anticipated', *Journal of Marketing Education*, vol. 21, no. 3, pp. 206–16.

Smith, S, Medendorp, CL, Ranck, S, Morrison, K and Kopfman, J (1994) 'The prototypical features of the ideal professor from the female and male undergraduate perspective: the role of verbal and nonverbal communication', *Journal on Excellence in College Teaching*, vol. 5, no. 2, pp. 5–22.

Southgate, EL (2000) 'Remembering school: mapping continuities in power, subjectivity and emotion in stories of Australian school life', Ph. D. thesis, University of Newcastle.

Stefani, LA (1998) 'Assessment in partnership with learners', *Assessment and Evaluation in Higher Education*, vol. 23, no. 4, pp. 339–50.

Steinberg, DL (1997) 'All roads lead to . . . problems with discipline', in *A question of discipline: pedagogy, power, and the teaching of cultural studies*, eds JE Canaan and D Epstein, Westview Press, Boulder, CO, pp. 192–204.

Steinmetz, C (2006) '"Tertiary de-generation": what baby-boomer educators need to know', paper presented at the Australian Association for Research in Education International Education Research Conference: Engaging Pedagogies, Adelaide, November.

Stern, PN (1980) 'Grounded theory methodology', *Image*, vol. XII, no. 1.

Stronge, JH (2002) *Qualities of effective teachers*, Association for Supervision and Curriculum Development, Alexandria, VA.

Tang, C (1994) 'Effects of modes of assessment on students' preparation strategies', in *Improving student learning: theory and practice*, ed. G Gibbs, Oxford Centre for Staff and Learning Development, Oxford, pp. 151–70.

Tata, J (1999) 'Grade distributions, grading procedures, and students' evaluations of instructors: a justice perspective', *Journal of Psychology*, vol. 133, no. 3, pp. 263–71.

Teven, JJ and McCroskey, JC (1996) 'The relationship of perceived teacher caring with student learning and teacher evaluation', *Communication Education*, vol. 46, pp. 1–9.

Thibaut, J and Walker, L (1975) *Procedural justice: a psychological analysis*, Lawrence Erlbaum Associates, Hillsdale, NJ.

Trotter, E (2006) 'Student perceptions of continuous summative assessment', *Assessment and Evaluation in Higher Education*, vol. 31, no. 5, pp. 505–21.

University of South Australia (2010) *Assessment policies and procedures manual*, UniSA, Adelaide.

Volet, S and Mansfield, C (2006) 'Group work at university: significance of personal goals in the regulation strategies of students with positive and negative appraisals', *Higher Education Research and Development*, vol. 25, no. 4, pp. 341–56.

Walker, A (2001) 'British psychology students' perceptions of group-work and peer assessment', *Psychology Learning and Teaching*, vol. 1, no. 1, pp. 28–36.

Walkerdine, V (1990) *Schoolgirl fictions*, Verso, London.

Walsh, DJ and Maffei, MJ (1994) 'Never in a class by themselves: an examination of behaviors affecting the student–professor relationship', *Journal on Excellence in College Teaching*, vol. 5, no. 2, pp. 23–50.

Weaver, MR (2006) 'Do students value feedback? Student perceptions of tutors' written responses', *Assessment and Evaluation in Higher Education*, vol. 31, no. 3, pp. 379–94.

Webb, NM (1995) 'Group collaboration in assessment: multiple objectives, processes, and outcomes', *Educational Evaluation and Policy Analysis*, vol. 17, no. 2, pp. 239–61.

Weick, KE (1988) 'Enacted sensemaking in crisis situations', *Journal of Management Studies*, vol. 25, no. 4, pp. 305–17.

White, F, Lloyd, H, Kennedy, G and Stewart, C (2005) 'An investigation of undergraduate students' feelings and attitudes towards group work and group assessment', paper presented at the HERDSA Higher Education in a Changing World Conference, Sydney, July.

Williams, E (1992) 'Student attitudes towards approaches to learning and assessment, *Assessment and Evaluation in Higher Education*, vol. 17, no. 1, pp. 45–58.

Winter, JK, Neal, JC and Waner, KK (1996) 'Student and instructor use of comments on business communication papers', *Business Communication Quarterly*, vol. 59, no. 4, pp. 56–68.

Index